Seven Key Question Words

When you arrive in **France** (frah$^{(n)}$-s) or **Québec** (kay-bek), the very first thing you will need to do is to ask questions — "Where is the train station?" "Where can I exchange money?" "Where **(où)** (oo) is the lavatory?" "**Où** is the restaurant?" "**Où** do I catch a taxi?" "**Où** is a good hotel?" "**Où** is my luggage?" — and the list will go on and on for the entire length of your visit. In French, there are SEVEN KEY QUESTION WORDS to learn. For example, the seven key question words will help you to find out exactly what you are ordering in a restaurant before you order it — and not after the surprise (or shock!) arrives. Take a few minutes to study and practice saying the seven basic question words listed below. Notice that "what" and "who" are only differentiated by one letter, so be sure not to confuse them. Then cover the French words with your hand and fill in each of the blanks with the matching **mot** (mow) [word] **français** (frah$^{(n)}$-say) [French].

1.	(oo) **OÙ**	=	WHERE	où, où, où, où, où
2.	(key) **QUI**	=	WHO	QUI, QUI, QUI, QUI, QUI
3.	(kuh) **QUE/QU'**	=	WHAT	QUE/QU' QUE QUE QUE
4.	(poor-kwah) **POURQUOI**	=	WHY	POURQUOI, POURQUOI, POURQUOI, POURQUOI
5.	(kah$^{(n)}$) **QUAND**	=	WHEN	QUAND, QUAND, QUAND, QUAND, QUAND
6.	(ko-mah$^{(n)}$) **COMMENT**	=	HOW	COMMENT, COMMENT, COMMENT, COMMENT
7.	(kohm-bee-yen) **COMBIEN**	=	HOW MUCH	COMBIEN, COMBIEN, COMBIEN, COMBIEN

Now test yourself to see if you really can keep these **mots** *(mow)* (words) straight in your mind. Draw lines between the French **et** *(ay)* (and) English equivalents below.

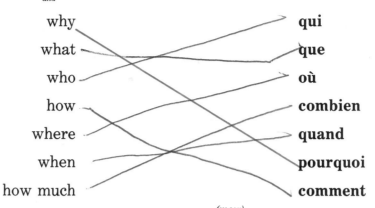

why	**qui**
what	**que**
who	**où**
how	**combien**
where	**quand**
when	**pourquoi**
how much	**comment**

Examine the following questions containing these **mots** *(mow)*. Practice the sentences out loud many times **et** *(ay)* (and) then quiz yourself by filling in the blanks below with the correct question **mot.**

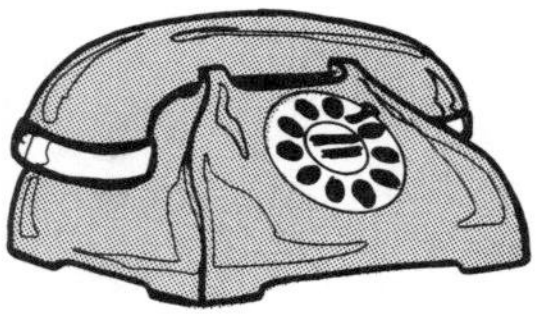

(oo) (ay) (luh) (tay-lay-phone)
Où est le téléphone?
Where is the telephone?

(key) (ess)
Qui est-ce?
Who is it?

(kohm-bee-yen) (ess)
Combien est-ce?
How much is it?

(kah$^{(n)}$) (luh) (tra$^{(n)}$) (ah-reev-teel)
Quand le train arrive-t-il?
When the train does it arrive?

(kess) (key) (suh) (pahss)
Qu'est-ce qui se passe?
What's happening?

(ko-mah$^{(n)}$) (ay) (lah) (sah-lahd)
Comment est la salade?
How is the salad?

(kess) (kuh) (say)
Qu'est-ce que c'est?
What is it?

(poor-kwah) (luh) (tra$^{(n)}$) (nah-reev-teel) (pah)
Pourquoi le train n'arrive-t-il pas?
Why doesn't it arrive?

1. Comment **est la salade?**
2. ________________ **est-ce?**
3. ________________ **est-ce qui se passe?**
4. ________________ **est le téléphone?**
5. ________________ **le train n'arrive-t-il pas?**
6. ________________ **est-ce?**
7. ________________ **le train arrive-t-il?**
8. ________________ **est-ce que c'est?**

Où will be your most used question **mot,** so let's concentrate on it. **Répétez** *(ray-pay-tay)* (repeat) the following French sentences aloud. Then write out each sentence without looking at the **exemple.** *(eg-zahm-pluh)* If you don't succeed on the first try, don't give up. Just practice each sentence until you are able to do it easily. Don't forget that **"qu"** is pronounced like "k" and **"est-ce"** like "ess." Also, in French, the letter **"h"** is silent and **"th"** is pronounced like "t."

Où sont (soh$^{(n)}$) { **les cabinets?** (lay) (kah-bee-nay) / **les toilettes?** (twah-let)

Où est le taxi? (ay) (luh) (tahx-ee)

Où est l'autobus? (ay) (low-toe-boos)

Où est le taxi

OÙ SONT LES TOILETTE

Où est le taxi?

Où est le restaurant? (ay) (luh) (res-toe-rah$^{(n)}$)

Où est la banque? (lah) (bah$^{(n)}$k)

Où est l'hôtel? (low-tell)

OÙ EST LE RESTAURANT OÙ EST LA BANQUE OÙ EST L'HÔTEL

Oui (wee) *yes*, many of the **mots** (mow) which look like **anglais** (ah$^{(n)}$-glay) *English* are also **français** (frah$^{(n)}$-say) *French*. Since **français et** (ay) **anglais** share many words, your work here **est** (ay) *is* simpler. You will be amazed at the number of **mots** which are **identiques** (ee-dah$^{(n)}$-teak) *identical* (or almost **identiques**). Of course, they do not always sound the same when spoken by a French person, but the **similarité** (see-mee-lar-ee-tay) *similarity* will certainly surprise you. Listed below are five "free" **mots** beginning with "A" to help you get started. Be sure to say each **mot** aloud **et** (ay) then write out the **mot français** (frah$^{(n)}$-say) in the blank to the right.

☑ **l'accident** *(lack-see-dah$^{(n)}$)*	accident	______
☑ **l'addition** *(lah-dee-see-oh$^{(n)}$)*	the bill in a restaurant	______
☑ **l'admission** *(lahd-mee-see-oh$^{(n)}$)*	admission	______
☑ **l'adresse** *(lah-dress)*	address	l'adresse
☑ **aidez-moi!** *(ay-day-mwah)*	aid me! help me!	______

Free mots like these will appear at the bottom of the following pages in a yellow color band. They are easy — enjoy them!

Step 2

"the," "a," "some"

All of these words mean "the" in **français**:

(luh) **le**	(lah) **la**	**l'**	(lay) **les**

(gar-soh$^{(n)}$) **le garçon:**	the boy	(gar-soh$^{(n)}$) **les garçons:**	the boys
(fee-yah) **la fille:**	the girl	(fee-yah) **les filles:**	the girls
(lome) **l'homme:**	the man	(lay-zome) **les hommes:**	the men

These two words mean "a" or "an":

(uh$^{(n)}$) **un**	(ewn) **une**

These words mean "some":

(dew) **du**	(duh lah) **de la**	(duh) **de l'**	(day) **des**

(tra$^{(n)}$) **un train:**	a train
(uh-nome) **un homme:**	a man
(fahm) **une femme:**	a woman
(sah-lahd) **une salade:**	a salad

(soo-kruh) **du sucre:**	some sugar
(moo-tard) **de la moutarde:**	some mustard
(la$^{(n)}$-tay-ray) **de l'intérêt:**	some interest
(fwee) **des fruits:**	some fruits

Le français (frah$^{(n)}$-say) (French) has multiple **mots** for "the," "a" and "some," but there **est** (ay) (is) no need to worry about it. Just make a choice **et** (ay) remember to use one of these **mots** when you mean "the," "a" **ou** (oo) (or) "some."

Step 3

Les Choses (lay) (showz)

things

Before you proceed **avec** (ah-vek) (with) this step, situate yourself comfortably in your living room. Now look around you. Can you name the things which you see in this **pièce** (pea-ess) (room) in **français?** Probably you can guess **la lampe** (lahmp) and maybe even **la chaise** (shehz)**.** Let's learn the rest of them. After practicing these **mots** out loud, write them in the blanks below **et** (ay) on the next page.

le tableau (tah-blow) = the picture *le tableau* ______________

le plafond (plah-foh$^{(n)}$) = the ceiling ______________

- ☑ **l'alcool** *(lahl-kohl)* .... alcohol ______________
- ☐ **les Alpes** *(lay zahlp)* .... the Alps ______________
- ☐ **américain** *(ah-may-ree-ka$^{(n)}$)* .... American ______________
- ☐ **l'animal** *(lah-nee-mawl)* .... animal ______________
- ☐ **l'appartement** *(lah-par-teh-mah$^{(n)}$)* ..... apartment ______________

le coin *(kwa$^{(n)}$)* = the corner ____________

la fenêtre *(fuh-net-ruh)* = the window ____________

la lampe *(lahmp)* = the lamp ____________

la lumière *(lew-mee-air)* = the light ____________

le canapé *(kah-nah-pay)* = the sofa ____________

la chaise *(shehz)* = the chair ____________

le tapis *(tah-pee)* = the carpet ____________

la table *(tahb-luh)* = the table la table

la porte *(port)* = the door ____________

la pendule *(pah$^{(n)}$-dewl)* = the clock ____________

le rideau *(ree-doe)* = the curtain ____________

le mur *(mewr)* = the wall ____________

You will notice that the correct form of **le, la ou** *(oo)* **les** is given **avec** *(ah-vek)* (with) each noun. This is for your information — just remember to use one of them. Now open your book to the first page **avec** the stick-on labels. Peel off the first 14 labels **et** *(ay)* proceed around the **pièce,** *(pea-ess)* (room) labeling these items in your home. This will help to increase your French **mot** power easily. Don't forget to say **le mot** as you attach each label.

Now ask yourself, **"Où est le** *(luh)* **tableau?"** *(tah-blow)* **et** point at it while you answer, **"Voilà** *(vwah-lah)* (there is) **le tableau."** Continue on down the **liste** *(least)* (list) until you feel comfortable with these new **mots.** Say, **"Où est le plafond?"** *(plah-foh$^{(n)}$)* Then **répondez,** *(ray-poh$^{(n)}$-day)* (respond) **"Voilà le** *(luh)* **plafond,"** and so on. When you can identify all the items on the **liste,** *(least)* you will be ready to move on.

Now, starting on the next page, let's learn some basic parts of the house.

- ☐ **l'appétit** *(lah-pay-tee)* . . . . appetite ____________
- ☐ **l'arrêt** *(lah-ray)* . . . . stop, arrest ____________
- ☐ **l'arrivée** *(lah-ree-vay)* . . . . arrival ____________
- ☐ **l'attention** *(lah-tah$^{(n)}$-see-oh$^{(n)}$)* . . . . attention ____________
- ☐ **l'auteur** *(low-tur)* . . . . author ____________

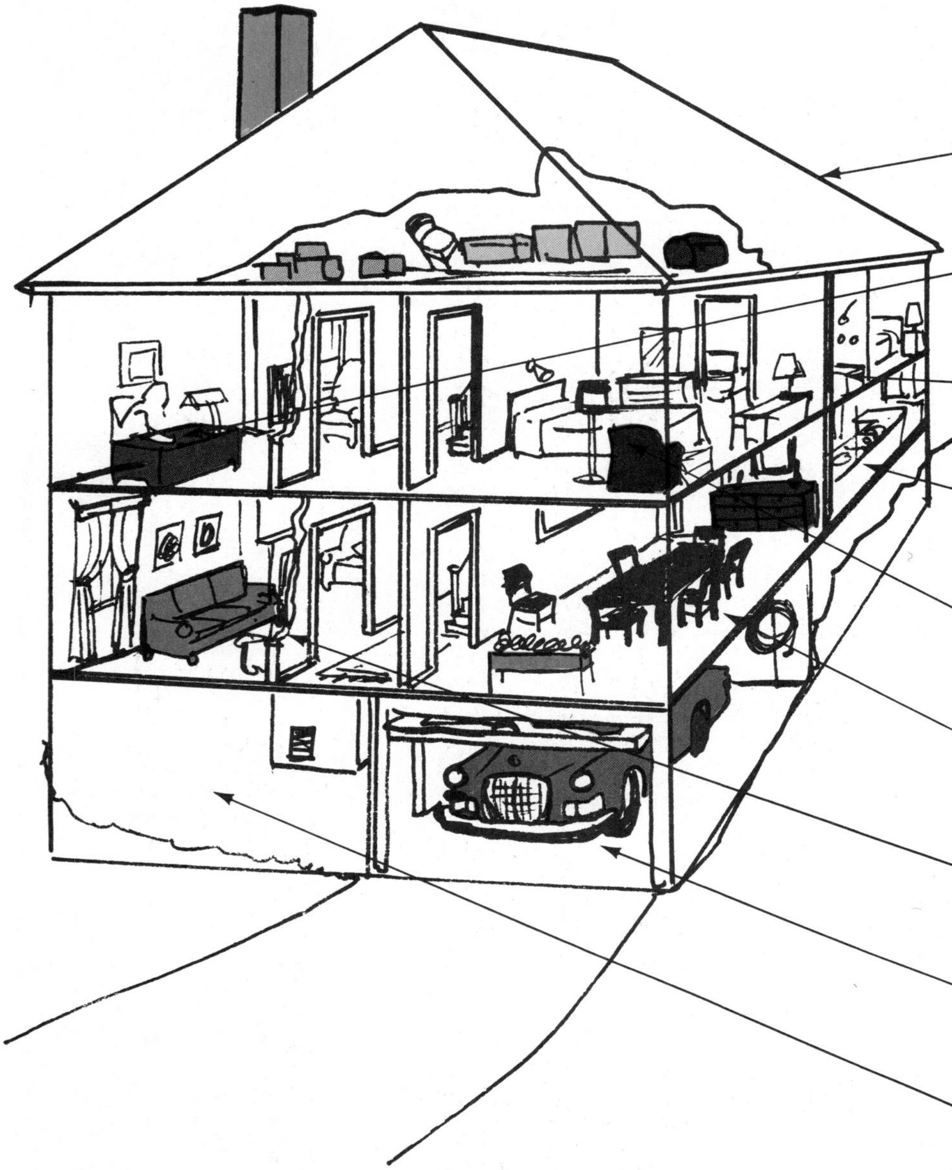

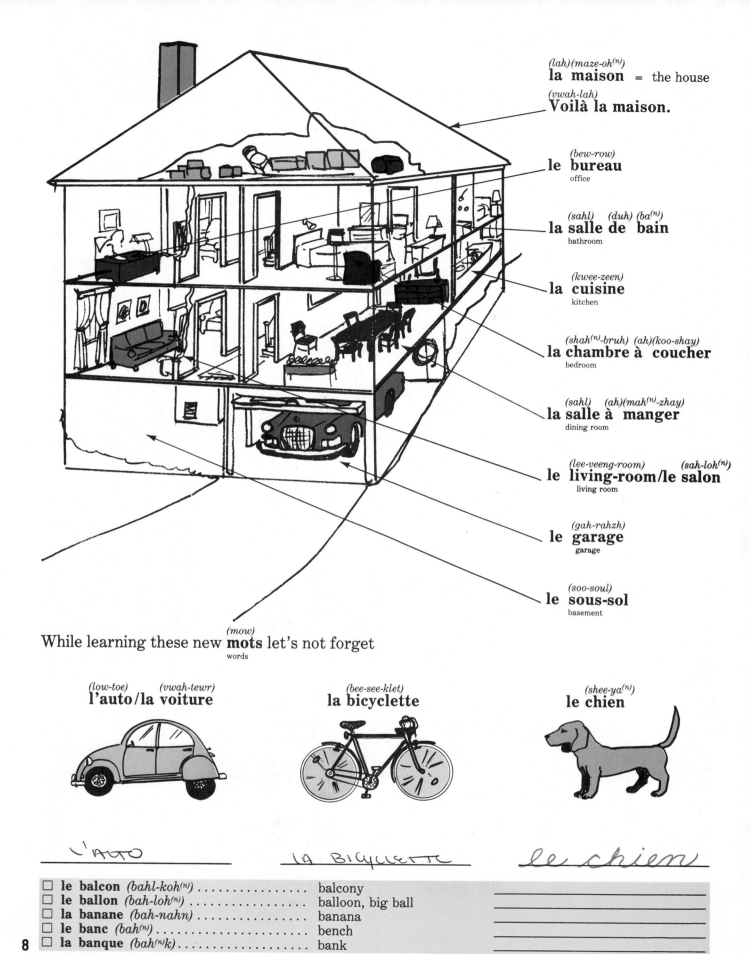

(lah)(maze-oh$^{(n)}$)
la maison = the house

(vwah-lah)
Voilà la maison.

(bew-row)
le bureau
office

(sahl) (duh) (ba$^{(n)}$)
la salle de bain
bathroom

(kwee-zeen)
la cuisine
kitchen

(shah$^{(n)}$-bruh) (ah)(koo-shay)
la chambre à coucher
bedroom

(sahl) (ah)(mah$^{(n)}$-zhay)
la salle à manger
dining room

(lee-veeng-room) (sah-loh$^{(n)}$)
le living-room/le salon
living room

(gah-rahzh)
le garage
garage

(soo-soul)
le sous-sol
basement

While learning these new *(mow)* **mots** (words) let's not forget

(low-toe) (vwah-tewr)
l'auto/la voiture

l'auto

(bee-see-klet)
la bicyclette

la bicyclette

(shee-ya$^{(n)}$)
le chien

le chien

- ☐ **le balcon** *(bahl-koh$^{(n)}$)* . . . . balcony
- ☐ **le ballon** *(bah-loh$^{(n)}$)* . . . . balloon, big ball
- ☐ **la banane** *(bah-nahn)* . . . . banana
- ☐ **le banc** *(bah$^{(n)}$)* . . . . bench
- ☐ **la banque** *(bah$^{(n)}$k)* . . . . bank

(shah)
le chat
cat

(zhar-da$^{(n)}$)
le jardin
garden

(koo-ree-ay)
le courrier
mail

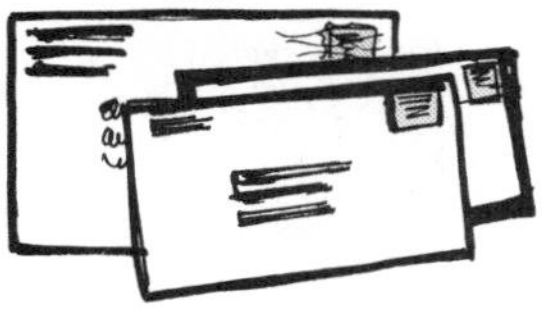

le chat ~~shah~~ ______ le jardin ______ ______

(bwaht) (oh) (let-ruh)
la boîte aux lettres
mail box

(fluhr)
les fleurs
flowers

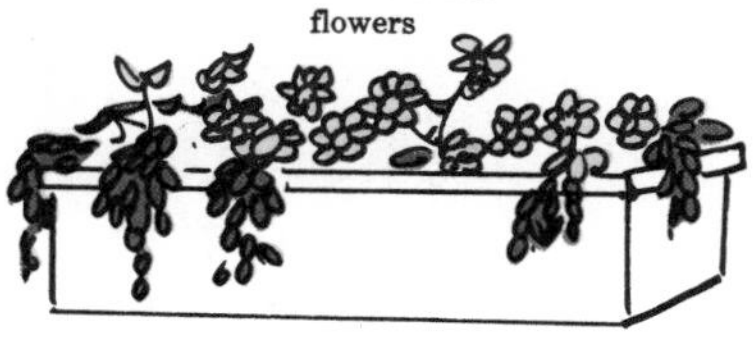

(so-net)
la sonnette
door bell

la boite aux lettres ______ les fleurs ______ ______

Peel off the next set of labels *(ay)* **et** wander through your *(maze-oh$^{(n)}$)* **maison** learning these new *(mow)* **mots.**

Granted, it will be somewhat difficult to label your **chien, chat ou fleurs,** but use your *(ee-mah-zhee-nah-see-oh$^{(n)}$)* **imagination.**

Again, practice by asking yourself, **"Où est le jardin?"** et *(ray-poh$^{(n)}$-day)* **répondez,** **"Voilà le jardin."**

Où est

☐ **le bifteck** *(beef-tek)*	beefsteak	______
☐ **le biscuit** *(bee-skwee)*	cookie	______
☐ **la bouteille** *(boo-tay)*	bottle	______
☐ **bref** *(brehf)*	brief, short	______
☐ **brillant** *(bree-yah$^{(n)}$)*	brilliant, sparkling	______

Step 4

Un, deux, trois (uh(n)) (duh) (twah)
one two three

This is part of a little rhyme that **les enfants** (ah(n)-fah(n)) children **français récitent** (ray-seat) recite:

(uh(n)) (duh) (twah) **Un, deux, trois** one two three	(zhuh) (vay) (dah(n)) (lay) (bwah) **je vais dans les bois** I go into the woods
(kah-truh) (sank) (sees) **Quatre, cinq, six** four five six	(kuh-year) (day) (sir-eez) **cueillir des cerises.** to pick some cherries

For some reason, numbers are not the easiest thing to learn, but just remember how important they are in everyday **conversation** (koh(n)-vair-sah-see-oh(n)) conversation**.** How could you tell someone your phone number, your address or your hotel room if you had no numbers. And think of how difficult it would be if you could not understand the time, the price of an apple or the correct bus to take. When practicing the **nombres** (nome-bruh) numbers below, notice the **similarités** (see-mee-lar-ee-tay) similarities between **quatre** (kah-truh) (4) and **quatorze** (kah-torz) (14), **sept** (set) (7) and **dix-sept** (deez-set) (17) **et** so on.

0	(zay-row) **zéro**			0	zéro, zéro, zéro
1	(uh(n)) **un**	11	(oh(n)z) **onze**	1	
2	(duh) **deux**	12	(dues) **douze**	2	
3	(twah) **trois**	13	(trehz) **treize**	3	
4	(kah-truh) **quatre**	14	(kah-torz) **quatorze**	4	
5	(sank) **cinq**	15	(ka(n)z) **quinze**	5	
6	(sees) **six**	16	(says) **seize**	6	
7	(set) **sept**	17	(deez-set) **dix-sept**	7	
8	(wheat) **huit**	18	(deez-wheat) **dix-huit**	8	
9	(nuf) **neuf**	19	(deez-nuf) **dix-neuf**	9	
10	(dees) **dix**	20	(va(n)) **vingt**	10	

- ☐ **la capitale** *(kah-pee-tahl)* .... capital
- ☐ **la cathédrale** *(kah-tay-drahl)* .... cathedral
- ☐ **le cendrier** *(sah(n)-dree-ay)* .... ashtray (cinders)
- ☐ **le centre** *(sah(n)-truh)* .... center
- ☐ **le champagne** *(shah(n)-pan-yuh)* .... champagne

(ew-tee-lee-zay) **Utilisez** (use) these *(nome-bruh)* **nombres** on a daily basis. Count to yourself *(ah(n))* **en français** when you brush your teeth, exercise, *(oo)* **ou** (or) commute to work. Now fill in the following blanks according to the **nombres** given in parentheses.

Note: This is a good time to start learning these two important phrases.

(zhuh) (voo-dray) **Je voudrais**	=	I would like ______________
(new) (voo-dree-oh(n)) **Nous voudrions**	=	we would like ______________

(zhuh) (voo-dray) **Je voudrais**	quinze (15)	*(fuh-yuh) (duh) (pah-pee-ay)* **feuilles de papier.** sheets of paper	*(kohm-bee-yen)* **Combien?**	quinze (15)
Je voudrais	Dix (10)	*(kart) (pohs-tall)* **cartes postales.** postcards	**Combien?**	Di (10)
Je voudrais	onze (11)	*(ta(n)-bruh-post)* **timbres-poste.** stamps	**Combien?**	onze (11)
Je voudrais	Huit (8)	*(lee-truh) (day-sah(n)-s)* **litres d'essence.** liters of gas	**Combien?**	huit (8)
Je voudrais	un (1)	*(vair) (duh) (zhew) (door-ah(n)zh)* **verre de jus d'orange.** glass of orange juice	**Combien?**	un (1)
(new) (voo-dree-oh(n)) **Nous voudrions**	TWAH (3)	*(tahs) (duh) (tay)* **tasses de thé.** cups of tea	**Combien?**	______ (3)
Nous voudrions	quatre (4)	*(tee-kay) (doe-toe-boos)* **tickets d'autobus.** bus tickets	**Combien?**	______ (4)
Nous voudrions	deux (2)	*(bee-air)* **bières.** beers	**Combien?**	______ (2)
Je voudrais	______ (12)	*(uh) (fray)* **oeufs frais.** eggs fresh	**Combien?**	______ (12)
Nous voudrions	______ (6)	*(lee-vruh) (duh) (vee-ah(n)d)* **livres de viande.** pounds of meat	**Combien?**	______ (6)
Nous voudrions	SANK (5)	*(vair) (doe)* **verres d'eau.** glasses of water	**Combien?**	______ (5)
Je voudrais	______ (7)	*(vair) (duh) (va(n))* **verres de vin.** glasses of wine	**Combien?**	______ (7)
Nous voudrions	______ (9)	*(lee-vruh) (duh) (buhr)* **livres de beurre.** pounds of butter	**Combien?**	______ (9)

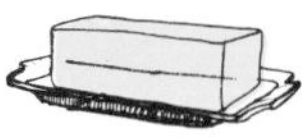

- ☐ **le changement** *(shah(n)-zhuh-mah(n))* . . . . change ______________
- ☐ **le chèque** *(shek)* . . . . bank check ______________
- ☐ **le chocolat** *(show-ko-lah)* . . . . chocolate ______________
- ☐ **le coiffeur** *(kwah-fur)* . . . . hairdresser ______________
- ☐ **la communication** *(ko-mew-nee-kah-see-oh(n))* . communication ______________

Now see if you can translate the following thoughts into **français.** (lay) (ray-poh(n)s) **Les réponses** [answers] are at the bottom of the (pahzh) **page.**

1. I would like seven postcards.

____

2. I would like one beer.

Je voudrais une bière.

3. We would like two glasses of water.

____

4. We would like three bus tickets.

____

Review **les nombres** 1 **à** [to] 20 **et** answer the following (kehs-tee-oh(n)) **questions** aloud, **et** then write the (ray-poh(n)s) **réponses** in the blank spaces to the left.

(kohm-bee-yen) (duh) (tahb-luh) (ee) **Combien de tables y** [are] (ah-teel) (ee-see) **a-t-il** [there] **ici?** [here]

trois

(lahmp) (ee) **Combien de lampes y** (ah-teel) (ee-see) **a-t-il ici?**

____

(shehz) **Combien de chaises y a-t-il ici?**

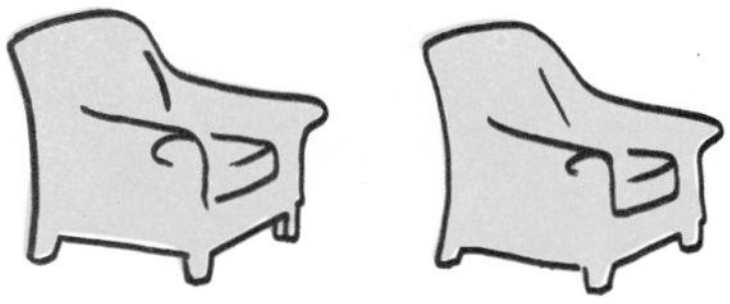

____

RÉPONSES CORRECTES

1. **Je voudrais sept cartes postales.**
2. **Je voudrais une bière.**
3. **Nous voudrions deux verres d'eau.**
4. **Nous voudrions trois tickets d'autobus.**

Combien de *(duh)* **pendules** *(pah$^{(n)}$-dewl)* **y** *(ee)* **a-t-il** *(ah-teel)* **ici?**

______

Combien de fenêtres *(fuh-net-ruh)* **y a-t-il ici?**

une

Combien de personnes *(pear-sohn)* **y a-t-il ici?**

______

Combien d'hommes *(dome)* **y a-t-il ici?**

______

Combien de femmes *(fahm)* **y a-t-il ici?**

______

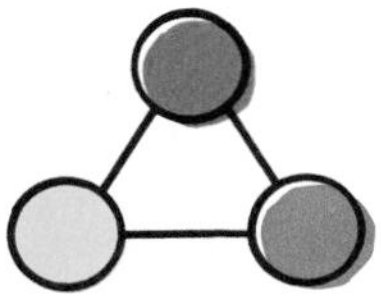

Les *(lay)* Couleurs *(koo-luhr)*

colors

Step 5

Les couleurs sont *(soh$^{(n)}$)* (are) the same **en** *(ah$^{(n)}$)* (in) **France** *(frah$^{(n)}$-s)* **et au** *(oh)* (in) **Québec** *(kay-bek)* as **en** *(ah$^{(n)}$)* **Amérique** *(nah-may-reek)*—they just have different **noms** *(noh$^{(n)}$)* (names). You can easily recognize **violet** *(vee-oh-lay)* as violet and **bleu** *(bluh)* as blue. So when you are invited to someone's **maison** *(maze-oh$^{(n)}$)* (house) **et** you want to bring flowers, you will be able to order the **couleur correcte** *(ko-rekt)* of flowers. (Contrary to American custom, **en** *(ah$^{(n)}$)* **Europe** *(nuh-rope)* **les fleurs** *(fluhr)* **rouges** *(roozh)* (red), **et** particularly **les roses** *(rose)* **rouges,** are only exchanged between lovers!) Let's learn the basic **couleurs** *(koo-luhr)*. Once you have read through **la liste** *(least)* on the next **page** *(pahzh)*, cover the **français avec** (with) your **main** *(ma$^{(n)}$)* (hand), **et** practice writing out the **français** next to the **anglais.** Notice the **similarités** *(see-mee-lar-ee-tay)* between **les mots en** *(ah$^{(n)}$)* **français** *(frah$^{(n)}$-say)* **et en** *(ah$^{(n)}$)* **anglais** *(nah$^{(n)}$-glay)*.

- ☐ **la compagnie** *(koh$^{(n)}$-pahn-yee)* .... company ______
- ☐ **le/la concierge** *(koh$^{(n)}$-see-airzh)* .... doorkeeper ______
- ☐ **la conversation** *(koh$^{(n)}$-vair-sah-see-oh$^{(n)}$)* ... conversation ______
- ☐ **le cousin** *(koo-za$^{(n)}$)* .... cousin (male) ______
- ☐ **la cousine** *(koo-zeen)* .... cousin (female) ______

(blah$^{(n)}$) **blanc**	=	white	*(bah-toe) (ay)* **Le bateau est blanc.** (bateau = boat)
(nwahr) **noir**	=	black	*(bawl)* **La balle est noire.**
(zhown) **jaune**	=	yellow	*(bah-nahn)* **La banane est jaune.**
(roozh) **rouge**	=	red	*(lee-vruh)* **Le livre est rouge.** (livre = book)
(bluh) **bleu**	=	blue bleu	*(low-toe)* **L'auto est bleue.**
(gree) **gris**	=	gray	*(lay-lay-fah$^{(n)}$)* **L'éléphant est gris.**
(mah-roh$^{(n)}$) **marron**	=	brown	*(shehz)* **La chaise est marron.** (chaise = chair)
(vair) **vert**	=	green	*(peh-looz) (vairt)* **La pelouse est verte.** (pelouse = grass)
(rose) **rose**	=	pink	*(fluhr)* **La fleur est rose.**
(mewl-tee-ko-lor) **multicolore**	=	multi-colored	*(lahmp)* **La lampe est multicolore.**

Now peel off the next **dix** *(dees)* labels **et** proceed to label these **couleurs** *(koo-luhr)* **dans** *(dah$^{(n)}$)* (in) your **maison** *(maze-oh$^{(n)}$)*.

Now let's practice using these **mots**.

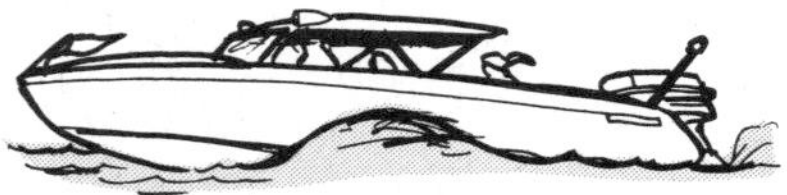

Où est le bateau blanc? — *(vwah-lah)* **Voilà** (there is) **le bateau** blanc.

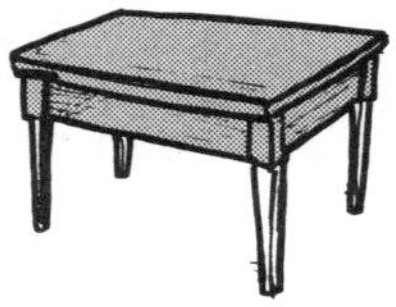

Où est la table grise? — **Voilà la table** ____________.

Où est la chaise marron? — **Voilà la chaise** ____________.

Où est la balle blanche? *(blah$^{(n)}$-shuh)* — **Voilà la balle** ____________.

Où est la lampe multicolore? — **Voilà la lampe** ____________.

Où est le livre rouge? — **Voilà le livre** ____________.

- ☐ **la dame** *(dahm)* . . . . lady ____________
- ☐ **la danse** *(dah$^{(n)}$-s)* . . . . dance ____________
- ☐ **décembre** *(day-sah$^{(n)}$m-bruh)* . . . . December ____________
- ☐ **la déclaration** *(day-klah-rah-see-oh$^{(n)}$)* . . . declaration ____________
- ☐ **le départ** *(day-par)* . . . . departure ____________

Où est la porte verte? *(vairt)* **Voilà la porte** ____________.

Où est la maison rose? **Voilà la maison** ____________.

Où est la banane jaune? **Voilà la banane** ____________.

Note: **En** *(ah$^{(n)}$)* **français,** *(frah$^{(n)}$-say)* the **verbe** *(vairb)* for "to have" **est "avoir."** *(ah-vwahr)*

j'ai *(zhay)* = I have ______________________ **nous avons** *(new) (zah-voh$^{(n)}$)* = we have ______________________

Let's review **je** *(zhuh)* (I) **voudrais** *(voo-dray)* (would like) **et nous** *(new)* (we) **voudrions** *(voo-dree-oh$^{(n)}$)* (would like) **et** learn **avoir.** *(ah-vwahr)* (to have) **Répétez** *(ray-pay-tay)* each sentence out loud.

Je voudrais un verre de bière. *(voo-dray) (zuh$^{(n)}$) (vair) (duh) (bee-air)*

Nous voudrions deux verres de vin. *(voo-dree-oh$^{(n)}$) (duh) (va$^{(n)}$)*

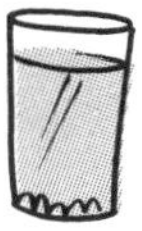

J'ai un verre de bière. *(zhay)*

Nous avons deux verres de vin. *(ah-voh$^{(n)}$)*

Je voudrais un verre d'eau. *(doe)*

Nous voudrions une salade. *(zewn) (sah-lahd)*

Nous avons une maison. *(zewn)*

J'ai une maison en Amérique. *(ah$^{(n)}$) (nah-may-reek)*

Nous voudrions avoir une auto. *(zah-vwahr) (oh-toe)*

Nous voudrions avoir une auto en Europe. *(uh-rope)*

J'ai une auto. *(oh-toe)*

Nous avons une auto en Europe. *(ah$^{(n)}$) (nuh-rope)*

Now fill in the following blanks **avec** the **forme correcte** *(form) (ko-rekt)* of **"avoir" ou "vouloir."** *(oo)* (or)

Nous avons ______________________ **trois autos.**
(we have)

______________________ **deux tickets d'autobus.**
(we would like)

______________________ **un tableau.**
(I have)

______________________ **sept cartes postales.**
(I would like)

- ☐ **déjà** *(day-zhah)* . . . . already ____________
- **— déjà vu** *(day-zhah vew)* . . . . already seen ____________
- ☐ **le désir** *(day-zeer)* . . . . desire ____________
- ☐ **la distance** *(dee-stah$^{(n)}$-s)* . . . . distance ____________
- ☐ **le docteur** *(doke-tur)* . . . . doctor ____________

Voilà a quick review of the **couleurs** *(koo-luhr)*. Draw lines between **les** *(lay)* **mots** *(mow)* **français** *(frah$^{(n)}$-say)* **et les couleurs correctes** *(ko-rekt)*. On your mark, get set, *GO!*

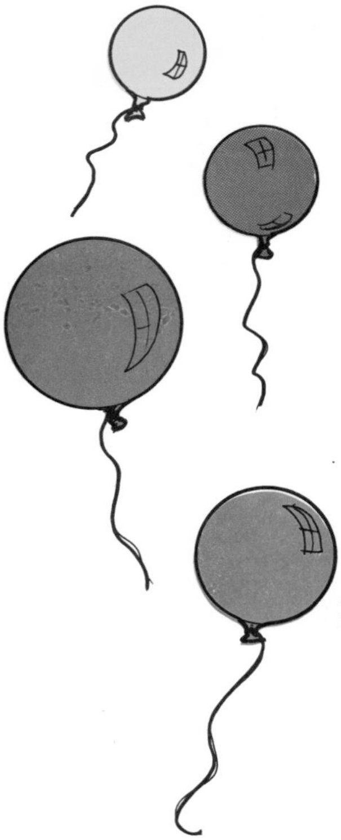

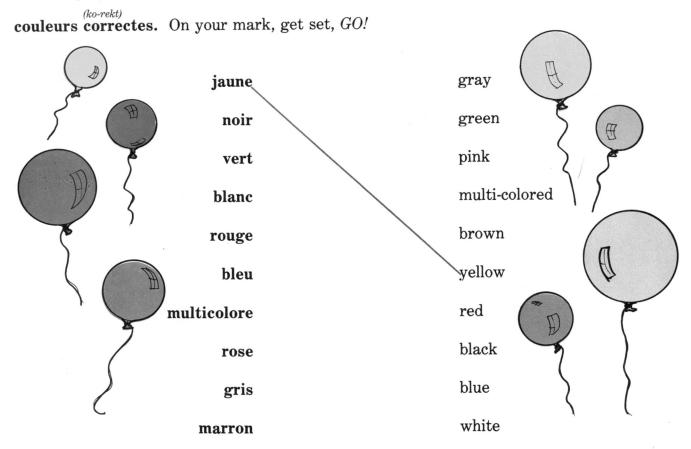

jaune	gray
noir	green
vert	pink
blanc	multi-colored
rouge	brown
bleu	yellow
multicolore	red
rose	black
gris	blue
marron	white

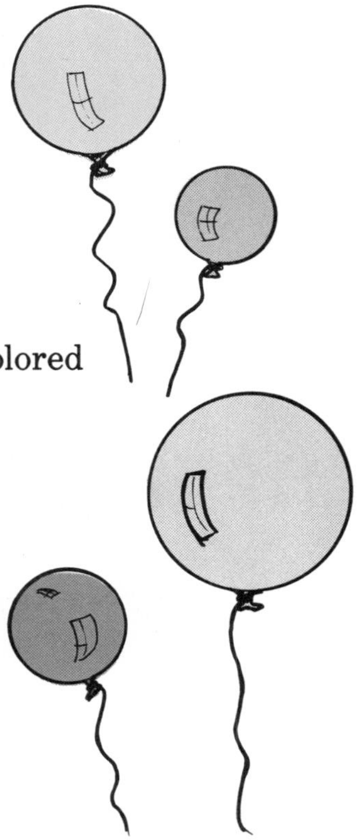

Where to place the accent in French need never be a problem. **Les** *(lay)* **mots français** *(frah$^{(n)}$-say)* are always accented on the last syllable. It's easy!

- ☐ **l'économie** *(lay-koh-noh-mee)* .... economy
- ☐ **l'entrée** *(lah$^{(n)}$-tray)* .... entry
- ☐ **est** *(est)* .... east
- ☐ **l'état** *(lay-tah)* .... state
  - **— Les Etats-Unis d'Amérique** *(lay-zay-tah-zoo-nee dah-may-reek)* The United States of America

Step 6

(lar-zhah$^{(n)}$)
L'Argent
money

Before starting this Step, go back **et** review Step 4. Make sure you can count to **vingt** (va$^{(n)}$) without looking back at **le livre** (lee-vruh). Let's learn the larger **nombres** (nome-bruh) now, so if something costs more than 20 **F** (frah$^{(n)}$) you will know exactly **combien** (kohm-bee-yen) it costs. After practicing aloud **les nombres français** 10 **à** 100 below, write these **nombres** in the blanks provided. Again, notice the **similarités** (see-mee-lahr-ee-tay) between **nombres** such as **quatre** (kah-truh) (4), **quatorze** (kah-torz) (14) and **quarante** (kah-rah$^{(n)}$t) (40).

10	(dees) **dix**	**(quatre + six = dix)**	**10** dix
20	(va$^{(n)}$) **vingt**	**(deux = 2)**	**20** ______
30	(trah$^{(n)}$t) **trente**	**(trois = 3)**	**30** ______
40	(kah-rah$^{(n)}$t) **quarante**	**(quatre = 4)**	**40** ______
50	(sang-kah$^{(n)}$t) **cinquante**	**(cinq = 5)**	**50** ______
60	(swah-sah$^{(n)}$t) **soixante**	**(six = 6)**	**60** ______
70	(swah-sah$^{(n)}$t-dees) **soixante-dix** (60 + 10)	**(sept = 7)**	**70** ______
80	(kah-truh-va$^{(n)}$) **quatre-vingts** (4x20)	**(huit = 8)**	**80** ______
90	(kah-truh-va$^{(n)}$-dees) **quatre-vingt-dix** (4x20 + 10)	**(neuf = 9)**	**90** ______
100	(sah$^{(n)}$) **cent**		**100** ______
1000	(meel) **mille**		**1000** ______

Now take a logical guess. **Comment** (ko-mah$^{(n)}$) would you write (**et** say) the following? **Les réponses** (ray-poh$^{(n)}$s) **sont** (are) at the bottom of **la** (lah) **page** (pahzh).

400 ______________________ 600 ______________________

2000 ______________________ 5300 ______________________

RÉPONSES

400 = quatre cents **2000 = deux mille**
600 = six cents **5300 = cinq mille trois cents**

The unit of currency **en France est** *(ay)* **le franc** *(frah(n))* **français** *(frah(n)-say)*, abbreviated **F**. Bills are called **billets** *(bee-ay)* **et** coins are called **monnaie** *(mo-nay)*. Just as **un** *(uh(n))* **dollar** *(doe-lahr)* **américain** *(ah-may-ree-ka(n))* can be broken down into 100 pennies, **un franc** *(frah(n))* **français** can be broken down into 100 **centimes** *(sah(n)-teem)*. A coin is called **une** *(ewn)* **pièce** *(pea-ess)* **de monnaie** *(mo-nay)* **et** bills can also be referred to as **papier-monnaie** *(pah-pee-ay mo-nay)*. Let's learn the various kinds of **billets** *(bee-ay)* **et monnaie** *(mo-nay)*. Always be sure to practice each **mot** out loud. You might want to exchange some money **maintenant** *(ma(n)-tuh-nah(n))* (now) so that you can familiarize yourself **avec** the various types of **argent** *(ar-zhah(n))* (money).

Billets

un *(uh(n))* **billet** *(bee-ay)* **de dix** *(dee)* (10) **francs** *(frah(n))* (francs)

un billet de cinquante *(sang-kah(n)t)* (50) **francs**

un billet de cent francs

un billet de cinq cents francs

Monnaie

une *(ewn)* **pièce** *(pea-ess)* **d'un** *(duh(n))* (1) **centime** *(sah(n)-teem)* (centime)

une pièce de cinq (5) **centimes**

une pièce de dix (10) **centimes**

une pièce de vingt centimes

une pièce de cinquante centimes (un demi-franc)

une pièce d'un franc

une pièce de cinq francs

une pièce de dix francs

☐ **la fatigue** *(fah-teeg)*	fatigue, tiredness	________
—je suis fatigué *(zhuh swee fah-tee-gay)*	I am tired	________
☐ **la fête** *(feht)*	feast, festival	________
☐ **le festival** *(feh-stee-vahl)*	festival	________
☐ **le film** *(feelm)*	film	________

Review **les nombres dix** through **mille** again. *(ma(n)-tuh-nah(n))* **Maintenant,** (now) how do you say "twenty-two" *(oo)* **ou** "fifty-three" *(ah(n))* **en français?** You basically put **les nombres** together in a logical sequence, for example 78 (60 + 18) = **soixante-dix-huit.** (60 18) See if you can say **et** write out **les nombres** on this **page. Les réponses** *(soh(n))* **sont** at the bottom of **la page.**

a. 25 = ____________ (20 + 5)

b. 36 = ____________ (30 + 6)

c. 47 = ____________ (40 + 7)

d. 93 = ____________ (4 x 20 + 13)

e. 84 = ____________ (4 x 20 + 4)

f. 68 = soixante-huit (60 + 8)

g. 51 = ____________ (50 + 1)

h. 72 = ____________ (60 + 12)

To ask what something costs **en français,** one asks, *(kohm-bee-yen) (ess-kuh) (sah) (koot)* **"Combien est-ce que ça coûte?"**

(ma(n)-tuh-nah(n)) **Maintenant** answer the following questions based on **les nombres** in parentheses.

1. *(kohm-bee-yen) (ess-kuh) (sah) (koot)* **Combien est-ce que ça coûte?** (how much does it cost) *(sah) (koot)* **Ça coûte** (it costs) dix (10) **francs.**

2. **Combien est-ce que ça coûte? Ça coûte** ____________ (20) **francs.**

3. **Combien coûte le** *(lee-vruh)* **livre?** (how much costs) **Ça coûte** ____________ (17) **francs.**

4. **Combien coûte** *(low-toe)* **l'auto? Ça coûte** ____________ (2000) **francs.**

5. **Combien coûte le** *(feelm)* **film? Ça coûte** ____________ (5) **francs.**

6. **Combien coûte la** *(shah(n)-bruh)* **chambre? Ça coûte** ____________ (24) **francs.**

7. **Combien coûte le** *(tah-blow)* **tableau? Ça coûte** ____________ (923) **francs.**

RÉPONSES

a. **vingt-cinq**	f. **soixante-huit**	3. **dix-sept**
b. **trente-six**	g. **cinquante et un**	4. **deux mille**
c. **quarante-sept**	h. **soixante-douze**	5. **cinq**
d. **quatre-vingt-treize**	1. **dix**	6. **vingt-quatre**
e. **quatre-vingt-quatre**	2. **vingt**	7. **neuf cent vingt-trois**

Congratulations!

Step 7

Aujourd'hui, demain et hier

(oh-zhoor-dwee) **Aujourd'hui,** today *(duh-ma$^{(n)}$)* **demain** tomorrow **et** *(ee-air)* **hier** yesterday

(kah-lah$^{(n)}$-dree-ay) **Le calendrier** (calendar)						
Une *(suh-men)* **semaine** (week) *(ah)* **a** (has) **sept** *(zhoor)* **jours.** (days)						
lundi	**mardi**	**mercredi**	**jeudi**	**vendredi**	**samedi**	**dimanche**
1	**2**	**3**	**4**	**5**	**6**	**7**

(eel) **Il** (it) **est** (is) *(tray)* **très** (very) *(za$^{(n)}$-por-tah$^{(n)}$)* **important** to know the days of the week **et** the various parts of the day. Let's learn them. Be sure to say them aloud before filling in the blanks below. **Les** (the) *(frah$^{(n)}$-say)* **Français** (French) begin counting their week on Monday with **lundi.**

(lun-dee) **lundi** lundi	*(mar-dee)* **mardi** ______
(mare-kruh-dee) **mercredi** ______	*(zhuh-dee)* **jeudi** ______
(vah$^{(n)}$-druh-dee) **vendredi** ______	*(sahm-dee)* **samedi** ______
(dee-mah$^{(n)}$sh) **dimanche** ______	

If *(oh-zhoor-dwee)* **aujourd'hui est mercredi,** then *(duh-ma$^{(n)}$)* **demain est jeudi et** *(ee-air)* **hier** *(ay-tay)* **était** (was) **mardi. Maintenant,** you supply **les réponses correctes.** If **aujourd'hui est lundi,** then **demain est** ______ **et hier était** ______. **Ou,** if **aujourd'hui est lundi,** then ______ **est mardi et** hier **était dimanche.** *(kel)* **Quel** (what) *(zhoor)* **jour** (day) *(ess)* **est-ce** (is it) **aujourd'hui? Aujourd'hui** *(ay)* **est** ______.

(ma$^{(n)}$-tuh-nah$^{(n)}$) **Maintenant,** peel off the next **sept** labels **et** put them on a *(kah-lah$^{(n)}$-dree-ay)* **calendrier** you use every day. From **aujourd'hui** on, Monday **est "lundi."**

☐ **le filtre** *(feel-truh)*	filter	______
—**un café filtre** *(kah-fay feel-truh)*	filtered coffee	______
☐ **la fin** *(fa$^{(n)}$)*	end	______
☐ **le fontionnaire** *(foh$^{(n)}$-see-oh-nair)*	functionary, civil servant	______
☐ **le football** *(foot-bahl)*	soccer	______

There are **quatre** parts to each **jour.** (day)

morning	=	*(ma-ta$^{(n)}$)* **matin**	
afternoon	=	*(ah-pray-mee-dee)* **après-midi**	
evening	=	*(swahr)* **soir**	soir, soir, soir, soir, soir
night	=	*(nwee)* **nuit**	

Notice that the French days of the week are not capitalized as **en anglais.** *(ma$^{(n)}$-tuh-nah$^{(n)}$)* **Maintenant,** fill in the following blanks **et** then check your **réponses** at the bottom of **la page.**

a. Sunday morning = dimanche matin

b. Friday evening = ______

c. Saturday evening = ______

d. Monday morning = ______

e. Wednesday morning = ______

f. Tuesday afternoon = ______

g. Thursday afternoon = ______

h. Thursday night = ______

i. yesterday evening = ______

j. yesterday morning = ______

k. tomorrow evening = ______

l. tomorrow afternoon = ______

m. yesterday afternoon = ______

RÉPONSES

a. **dimanche matin**
b. **vendredi soir**
c. **samedi soir**
d. **lundi matin**
e. **mercredi matin**
f. **mardi après-midi**
g. **jeudi après-midi**
h. **jeudi nuit**
i. **hier soir**
j. **hier matin**
k. **demain soir**
l. **demain après-midi**
m. **hier après-midi**

So, **avec** merely **onze mots** you can specify any day of the **semaine** *(suh-men)* (week) **et** any time of the **jour.** *(zhoor)*

Les mots "aujourd'hui," *(oh-zhoor-dwee)* **"demain"** *(duh-ma(n))* **et "hier"** *(ee-air)* will be **très** *(tray)* **importants** *(za(n)-por-tah(n))* for you in making **réservations** *(ray-zair-vah-see-oh(n))* (reservations) **et rendez-vous,** *(rah(n)-day-voo)* (appointments) in getting **billets de théâtre** *(bee-yay) (duh) (tay-ah-truh)* (theater tickets) **et** many things you will wish to do. Knowing the parts of **le jour** will help you to learn **et** understand the various **salutations** *(sah-lew-tah-see-oh(n))* (greetings) **françaises** *(frah(n)-sez)* below. Practice these every day now until your trip.

good morning good afternoon	=	**bonjour** *(boh(n)-zhoor)*	______________
good evening	=	**bonsoir** *(boh(n)-swahr)*	______________
good night	=	**bonne nuit** *(bun) (nwee)*	bonne nuit
hi!	=	**salut** *(sah-lew)*	______________

Take the next **quatre** labels **et** stick them on the appropriate **choses** *(showz)* (things) in your **maison.** *(maze-oh(n))* How about the bathroom mirror **pour** *(poor)* (for) **"bonjour"? Ou** the front door **pour "bonsoir"? Ou** your alarm clock **pour "bonne nuit"?** Remember that whenever you enter small shops **et** stores **en France** you will hear the appropriate **salutation** *(sah-lew-tah-see-oh(n))* for the time of day. Don't be surprised. It is a **très** *(tray)* friendly **et** warm **coutume.** *(koo-tewm)* (custom) Everyone greets everyone **et** you should too, if you really want to enjoy **la France.** You **êtes** *(et)* (are) about one-fourth of your way through **le livre** *(lee-vruh)* **et c'est** *(say)* (it is) a good time to quickly review **les mots** you have learned before doing the crossword puzzle on the next **page. Amusez-vous** *(ah-mew-zay-voo)* (amuse yourself) **et bonne** *(bun)* (good) **chance.** *(shah(n)s)* (luck) **Ou** as we say **en anglais,** have fun and good luck.

RÉPONSES TO CROSSWORD PUZZLE (MOTS CROISÉS)

ACROSS

1. je voudrais
2. avec
3. avoir
4. Amérique
5. monnaie
6. ticket d'autobus
7. samedi
8. banque
9. dix-neuf
10. nuit
11. thé
12. vingt
13. mercredi
14. chaise
15. homme
16. cinquante
17. pendule
18. aujourd'hui
19. lumière
20. eau
21. cinq
22. quatre
23. et
24. voilà
25. comment
26. jaune
27. multicolore
28. trois
29. tableau
30. rideau

DOWN

1. jour
2. carte postale
3. noir
4. l'après-midi
5. plafond
6. réponse
7. salut
8. qui
9. qu'est-ce que c'est
10. argent
11. femme
12. un
13. mardi
14. nous avons
15. blanc
16. pourquoi
17. pièce
18. lampe
19. mur
20. rouge
21. vert
22. vendredi
23. maison
24. coin
25. gris
26. combien
27. quand
28. deux

CROSSWORD PUZZLE (MOTS CROISÉS)

(kwah-zay)

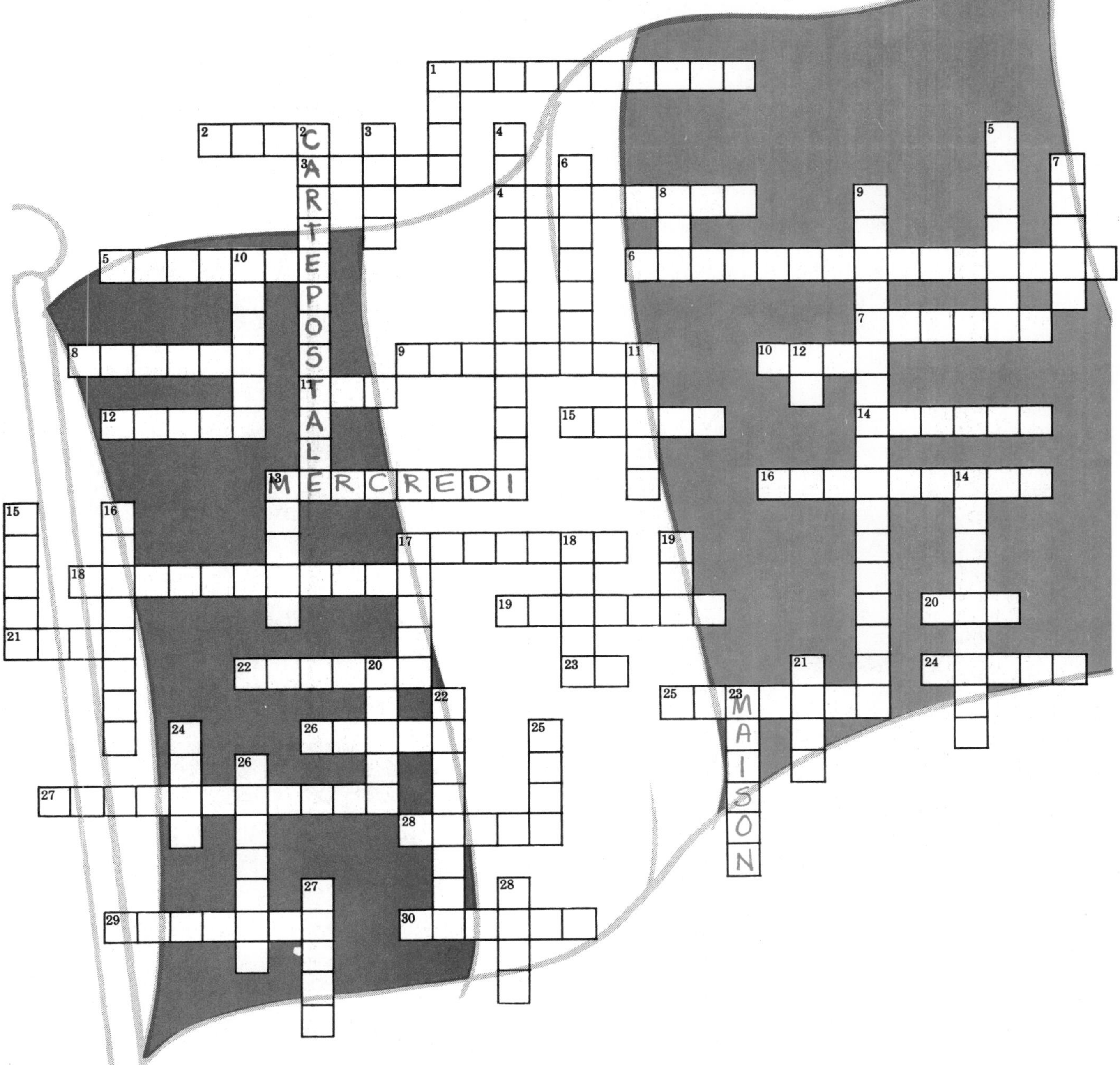

ACROSS

1. I would like
2. with
3. to have
4. America
5. coins
6. bus ticket
7. Saturday
8. bank
9. 19
10. night
11. tea
12. 20
13. Wednesday
14. chair
15. man
16. 50
17. clock
18. today
19. light
20. water
21. five
22. four
23. and
24. there is
25. how?
26. yellow
27. multi-colored
28. three
29. picture
30. curtain

DOWN

1. day
2. postcard
3. black
4. the afternoon
5. ceiling
6. response, answer
7. hi
8. who?
9. what is it?
10. money
11. woman
12. a (masculine)
13. Tuesday
14. we have
15. white
16. why?
17. room
18. lamp
19. wall
20. red
21. green
22. Friday
23. house
24. corner
25. gray
26. how much?
27. when?
28. two

Step 8

Dans, sur, sous . . .
(dah(n)) (sewr) (soo)
in, on, under

Les prépositions *(pray-poh-zee-see-oh(n))* **françaises** *(frah(n)-sez)* (words like "in," "on," "through" and "next to") **sont** (are) easy to learn **et** they allow you to be precise **avec** a minimum of effort. Instead of having to point **six** *(sees)* times at a piece of yummy pastry you wish to order, you can explain precisely which one you want by saying **il** *(eel)* (it) **est** (is) behind, in front of, next to, **ou** under the piece of pastry which the salesperson is starting to pick up. Let's learn some of these **petits** *(puh-tee)* (little) **mots** which **sont très** *(tray)* **similaires** *(see-mee-lair)* to **anglais.** Study the **exemples** *(eg-zah(n)-pluh)* below.

de* *(duh)* = out of/from	**à côté de*** *(ah koh-tay duh)* = next to	**sous** *(soo)* = under
dans *(dah(n))* = into/in		**au-dessus de*** *(oh-duh-sue-duh)* = over

L'homme entre *(ah(n)-truh)* (goes) **dans le nouvel** *(noo-vel)* (new) **hôtel** *(oh-tell)***.**

La femme vient *(vee-a(n))* (comes) **de l'excellent** *(lek-say-lah(n))* **hôtel.**

Le docteur *(doke-tur)* **est dans le bon** *(bun)* (good) **hôtel.**

Le nouveau *(noo-voh)* (new) **tableau est au-dessus de la table.**

Le nouveau tableau est à côté de l'horloge *(lor-lozh)* (large clock)**.**

Le chien gris est sous la table marron.

La table marron est au-dessus du *(dew)* **chien.**

L'horloge verte *(vairt)* **est au-dessus de la table.**

L'horloge verte est à côté du tableau.

*Remember that **de** sometimes combines with **la, le** or **les** to form **du** *(de + le)*, **de la, de l'** and **des** *(de + les)*.

- ☐ **la forme** *(form)* . . . . form, shape ______
- ☐ **la forêt** *(foh-ray)* . . . . forest ______
- ☐ **le foyer** *(fwah-yay)* . . . . home, hearth ______
- ☐ **franc/franche** *(frah(n)/frah(n)sh)* . . . . . frank, honest ______
- ☐ **le fruit** *(fwee)* . . . . fruit ______

Fill in the blanks below **avec les** **prépositions** *(pray-poh-zee-see-oh(n))* **correctes** according to the **images** *(ee-mahzh)* (pictures) on the previous **page.**

L'homme entre *(ah(n)-truh)* ________ **le nouvel hôtel.**

Le chien gris est sous **la table.**

L'horloge *(lor-lozh)* **verte** *(vairt)* **est** ________ **la table.**

Le docteur est ________ **le bon hôtel.**

L'horloge verte est ________ **du tableau.**

Le nouveau *(noo-voh)* **tableau est** ________ **la table.**

La table marron est ________ **le tableau.**

Le nouveau tableau est ________ **l'horloge.**

La femme *(fahm)* **vient** ________ **l'excellent hôtel.**

La table marron est ________ **l'horloge.**

Maintenant *(ma(n)-tuh-nah(n))*, **répondez aux** *(oh)* (to the) **questions** *(kehs-tee-oh(n))* based on **les** *(lay)* **images** *(zee-mahzh)* on the previous **page.**

Où est le docteur? ____

Où est le chien *(shee-ya(n))***?** ____

Où est la table? ____

Où est le tableau? ____

Que *(kuh)* **fait** *(fay)* (does) **la femme?** ____

Que fait *(fay)* (does) **l'homme?** ____

L'horloge est-elle (is it) **verte?** Oui, l'horloge est verte.

Le chien est-il (is it) **gris?** Oui,

- ☐ **la glace** *(glahs)* .... ice, ice cream ________
- ☐ **la galerie** *(gah-lur-ee)* .... gallery, long room ________
- ☐ **la géographie** *(zhay-oo-grah-fee)* .... geography ________
- ☐ **la gomme** *(gohm)* .... chewing gum, eraser ________
- ☐ **le gourmand** *(gour-mah(n))* .... gormand, glutton ________

Maintenant for some more practice **avec les prépositions françaises.**

(sewr) **sur** = on

(ah$^{(n)}$-truh) **entre** = between

(duh-vah$^{(n)}$) **devant** = in front of

(dare-ee-air) **derrière** = behind

Le verre *(vair)* **d'eau** *(doe)* **est** **sur** *(sewr)* **la table.**	**Le verre d'eau est ____________ la table.**
Le tableau multicolore est **sur** **le mur.**	**Le tableau multicolore est** sur **le mur.**
La lampe jaune est **derrière** *(dare-ee-air)* **la table.**	**La lampe jaune est ____________ la table.**
La table marron est **devant** *(duh-vah$^{(n)}$)* **le lit** *(lee)* (bed)**.**	**La table est ____________ le lit.**
La lampe jaune est **entre** *(ah$^{(n)}$-truh)* **la table et le lit.**	**La lampe jaune est ____________ la table et le lit.**

Répondez aux *(oh)* (to the) **questions,** based on **les images,** by filling in the blanks **avec les prépositions correctes.** Choose **les prépositions** from those you have just learned.

Où est le livre rouge?

Le livre rouge est ____________ la table marron.

Où est l'autobus bleu?

L'autobus bleu est ____________ l'hôtel gris.

- ☐ **le gourmet** *(gour-may)* . . . . gourmet, epicure ____________
- ☐ **le gouvernement** *(goo-vair-nuh-mah$^{(n)}$)* . government ____________
- ☐ **grand** *(grah$^{(n)}$)* . . . . big ____________
- ☐ **la grandeur** *(grah$^{(n)}$-dur)* . . . . greatness ____________
- ☐ **le guide** *(geed)* . . . . guide ____________

Où est le téléphone gris? Où est le tapis vert? Où est le tableau?
(tay-lay-phone) (gree) *(tah-pee) (vair)*

Le téléphone est ______________________ **le mur blanc.**

Le téléphone est ____________ **du tableau multicolore.**

Le téléphone est au-dessus de **la table noire.**

Le tapis vert est ______________________ **la table noire.**

Le tableau est _________________________ **le mur blanc.**

Maintenant, fill in each blank on **le château** *(shah-toe)* (castle) below **avec** the best possible **préposition.**

Les réponses correctes sont at the bottom of **la page. Amusez-vous.** (have fun)

1. ____________________________________

2. ________________________
3. ____________________________
4. ____________________
5. ________________
6. ____________________
7. _______________
8. devant
9. _________
10. ___________________________

RÉPONSES

1. **au-dessus de**	3. **derrière**	5. **dans**	7. **à côté de**	9. **sous**
2. **sur**	4. **entre**	6. **dans**	8. **devant**	10. **de**

Step 9

(zhah$^{(n)}$-vee-ay) (fay-vree-ay) (mars)
Janvier, février, mars

(oh$^{(n)}$) (sep-tah$^{(n)}$m-bruh) (ah-vreel) (zhoo-a$^{(n)}$) (no-vah$^{(n)}$m-bruh)
Trente jours ont septembre, avril, juin et novembre . . .
have

(suh-men) (mow-mah$^{(n)}$)
Sound familiar? You have learned the days of **la semaine,** so **maintenant c'est le moment**
it is
(mwah) (duh) (lah-nay) (tah$^{(n)}$)
to learn **les mois de l'année et** all kinds of **temps** which you might encounter on your
months of the year weather
(eg-zah$^{(n)}$-pluh) (tah$^{(n)}$)
holiday. For **exemple,** you ask about **le temps en français** just as you would **en anglais—**
(kel) (fay-teel) (kehs-tee-oh$^{(n)}$)
"Quel temps fait-il aujourd'hui?" Practice all the possible answers to this **question**
what weather does it do today
(pwee)
et puis write **les réponses** in the blanks below.
then

(kel) (tah$^{(n)}$) (fay-teel) (oh-zhoor-dwee)
Quel temps fait-il aujourd'hui?

(eel) (pluh)
Il pleut aujourd'hui. ____________________
rains

(nehzh)
Il neige aujourd'hui. Il neige aujourd'hui.
snows

(fay) (fray)
Il fait frais aujourd'hui. ____________________
cool

(fwah)
Il fait froid aujourd'hui. ____________________
cold

(boh)
Il fait beau aujourd'hui. ____________________
nice

(mow-vay)
Il fait mauvais aujourd'hui. ____________________
bad

(show)
Il fait chaud aujourd'hui. ____________________
hot

(dew) (broo-ee-yar)
Il fait du brouillard aujourd'hui. ____________________
foggy

(pwee)
Maintenant, practice **les mots** on the next **page** aloud **et puis** fill in the blanks with
then
(noh$^{(n)}$) (mwah)
les noms of **les mois et** the appropriate weather report. Notice that **en français,** the
names months
months of the year and the days of the week are not capitalized.

- ☐ **l'identification** *(lee-dah$^{(n)}$-tee-fee-kah-see-oh$^{(n)}$)* . identification ____________
- ☐ **l'île** *(leel)* . . . . island ____________
- ☐ **l'importance** *(la$^{(n)}$-por-tah$^{(n)}$s)* . . . . importance ____________
  - **— une chose importante** *(a$^{(n)}$-por-tah$^{(n)}$t)* . . . . . an important thing ____________
- ☐ **inacceptable** *(een-ahk-sep-tahb-luh)* . . . . unacceptable ____________

(ah$^{(n)}$)(zhah$^{(n)}$-vee-ay) **en janvier** ______ (en = in)	*(nehzh)* **Il neige en janvier.** ______
(fay-vree-ay) **en février** ______	*(oh-see)* **Il neige aussi en février.** ______ (aussi = also)
(mars) **en mars** en mars	*(pluh)* **Il pleut en mars.** ______
(ah-vreel) **en avril** ______	**Il pleut aussi en avril.** ______
(may) **en mai** ______	*(fay) (dew) (vah$^{(n)}$)* **Il fait du vent en mai.** ______ (vent = windy)
(zhoo-a$^{(n)}$) **en juin** ______	*(so-lay)* **Il fait du soleil en juin.** ______ (soleil = sunny)
(zhwee-ay) **en juillet** ______	*(boh)* **Il fait beau en juillet.** ______
(oot) **en août** ______	*(show)* **Il fait chaud en août.** Il fait chaud en août.
(sep-tah$^{(n)}$m-bruh) **en septembre** ______	*(broo-ee-yar)* **Il fait du brouillard en septembre.** ______ (brouillard = foggy)
(ok-toh-bruh) **en octobre** ______	*(fray)* **Il fait frais en octobre.** ______
(no-vah$^{(n)}$m-bruh) **en novembre** ______	*(mow-vay)* **Il fait mauvais en novembre.** ______
(day-sah$^{(n)}$m-bruh) **en décembre** ______	**Il fait froid en décembre.** ______

Maintenant, répondez aux questions based on **les images** to the right.

Quel temps fait-il en février? Il fait ______ (en = in)

Quel temps fait-il en avril? ______

Quel temps fait-il en mai? ______

Quel temps fait-il en août? ______

Quel temps fait-il aujourd'hui, beau ou mauvais? ______

- ☐ **impossible** *(a$^{(n)}$-poh-see-bluh)* . . . . impossible ______
  - **— C'est impossible!** *(say ta$^{(n)}$-poh-see-bluh)* . . It's impossible! ______
- ☐ **l'industrie** *(la$^{(n)}$-dew-stree)* . . . . industry ______
- ☐ **l'information** *(la$^{(n)}$-for-mah-see-oh$^{(n)}$)* . . . . . . information ______
- ☐ **l'ingénieur** *(la$^{(n)}$-zhay-nee-ur)* . . . . engineer ______

Maintenant, les saisons de l'année . . .
(say-zoh$^{(n)}$) saisons = seasons

(lee-vair) **l'hiver** (winter)	*(lay-tay)* **l'été** (summer)	*(loh-tone)* **l'automne** (autumn)	*(pra$^{(n)}$-tah$^{(n)}$)* **le printemps** (spring)

______	l'été	______	______
Il fait froid *(ah$^{(n)}$)(nee-vair)* **en hiver.**	**Il fait chaud** *(ah$^{(n)}$)(nay-tay)* **en été.**	**Il fait du vent** *(ah$^{(n)}$)(noh-tone)* **en automne.**	**Il pleut** *(oh)* **au printemps.**

At this point, **c'est** *(say)* (it is) **une** *(tewn)* (a) **bonne** *(bun)* (good) **idée** *(ee-day)* (idea) to familiarize yourself **avec les températures** *(tah$^{(n)}$-pay-rah-tewr)* (temperatures) **européennes** *(uh-roh-pay-yen)* (European)**.** Carefully read the typical weather forecasts below **et** study **le thermomètre** *(tair-moh-meh-truh)* (thermometer) because **les températures en Europe** *(uh-rope)* are calculated on the basis of Centigrade (not Fahrenheit).

Fahrenheit	Celsius	
212° F	100° C	*(low) (boo)* **l'eau bout** (boils)
98.6° F	37° C	**la température normale du sang** (of blood)
68° F	20° C	
32° F	0° C	**l'eau douce gèle** (water fresh freezes)
0° F	-17.8° C	**l'eau salée gèle** (water salt freezes)
-10° F	-23.3° C	

Le temps pour lundi 21 mars:

froid avec du vent
température: 5 degrés *(duh-gray)* (degrees)

Le temps pour mardi 18 juillet:

beau et chaud
température: 20 degrés

- ☐ **l'inscription** *(la$^{(n)}$-screep-see-oh$^{(n)}$)* ...... inscription ______
- ☐ **l'institut** *(la$^{(n)}$-stee-tew)* .... institute ______
- ☐ **intéressant** *(a$^{(n)}$-tay-ray-sah$^{(n)}$)* .... interesting ______
- ☐ **l'Italie** *(lee-tah-lee)* .... Italy ______
- — **italien** *(ee-tah-lee-a$^{(n)}$)* .... Italian ______

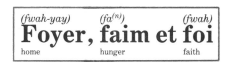

(fwah-yay) *(fa$^{(n)}$)* *(fwah)*
Foyer, faim et foi
home, hunger, faith

Just as we have the 3 "R's" **en anglais, en français** there are the 3 "F's" which help us to understand some of the basics of **la vie française.**
(vee) life, *(frah$^{(n)}$-sez)* French

Foyer

Faim

Foi

Study **les images** below **et puis** write out **les nouveaux mots** in the blanks which follow.
(pwee) then, *(noo-voh)* new

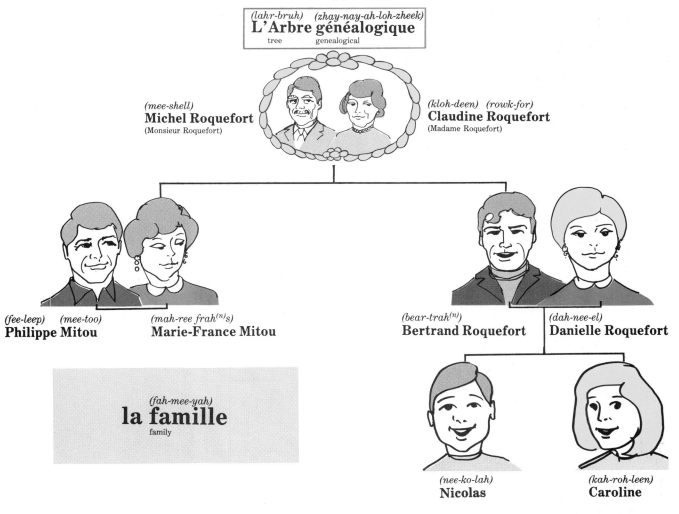

L'Arbre généalogique
(lahr-bruh) tree, *(zhay-nay-ah-loh-zheek)* genealogical

(mee-shell)
Michel Roquefort
(Monsieur Roquefort)

(kloh-deen) (rowk-for)
Claudine Roquefort
(Madame Roquefort)

(fee-leep) (mee-too)
Philippe Mitou

(mah-ree frah$^{(n)}$s)
Marie-France Mitou

(bear-trah$^{(n)}$)
Bertrand Roquefort

(dah-nee-el)
Danielle Roquefort

(fah-mee-yah)
la famille
family

(nee-ko-lah)
Nicolas

(kah-roh-leen)
Caroline

☐ **la jaquette** *(zhah-ket)*	woman's jacket	______
☐ **le Japon** *(zhah-poh$^{(n)}$)*	Japan	______
— **japonais** *(zhah-poh-nay)*	Japanese	______
☐ **le journal** *(zhoor-nahl)*	newspaper	______
☐ **La Joconde** *(zhoh-kohnd)*	Mona Lisa in the Louvre	______

(grah$^{(n)}$-pah-rah$^{(n)}$)
les grands-parents
grandparents

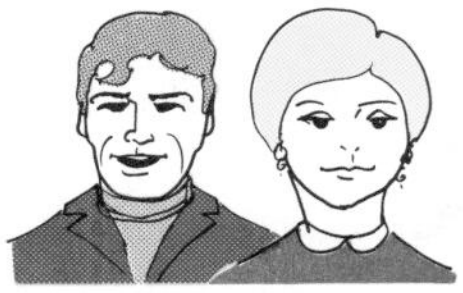

(pah-rah$^{(n)}$)
les parents
parents

(grah$^{(n)}$-pear)
le grand-père (grandfather) le grand-père

(grah$^{(n)}$-mare)
la grand-mère (grandmother) ____________________

(pear)
le père (father) ____________________

(mare)
la mère (mother) ____________________

(lay) (zah$^{(n)}$-fah$^{(n)}$)
les enfants
children

(pah-rah$^{(n)}$)
les parents
relatives

(fees)
le fils (son) ____________________

(fee-yah)
la fille (daughter) ____________________

(loh$^{(n)}$-kluh)
l'oncle (uncle) ____________________

(taunt)
la tante (aunt) ____________________

Le fils et la fille sont aussi frère *(frair)* (brother) et soeur *(suhr)* (sister).

Let's learn how to identify **la famille** *(fah-mee-yah)* (family) by **nom.** *(noh$^{(n)}$)* (name) Study the following **exemples.**

Comment (how) **s'appelle** *(sah-pell)* (is called) **le** (the) **père** (father)**?**

Le père s'appelle (is called) Bertrand.

Comment s'appelle (is called) **la mère?**

La mère s'appelle (is called) Danielle.

Maintenant you fill in the following blanks, **basés** *(bah-zay)* (based) **sur** *(sewr)* (on) **les images,** in the same manner.

Comment s'appelle le fils?

____________ **s'appelle** ____________.

Comment s'appelle ____________?

____________ **s'appelle** ____________.

☐ **juste** *(zhoost)*	fair, just	____________
☐ **la justice** *(zhoo-stees)*	justice	____________
☐ **le kilomètre** *(kee-loh-meh-truh)*	kilometer (=.624 miles)	____________
☐ **le kiosque** *(kee-ohsk)*	kiosk	____________
☐ **le kilo** *(kee-loh)*	kilo (=2.2 pounds)	____________

(kwee-zeen)
La cuisine
kitchen

Study all these **images et puis** practice saying **et** writing out **les mots.**

(lah)
Voilà la cuisine.

(ray-free-zhay-rah-tuhr)
le réfrigérateur

____

(kwee-zee-nee-air)
la cuisinière
stove

____

(va$^{(n)}$)
le vin

____

(bee-air)
la bière

____

(lay)
le lait

le lait

(buhr)
le beurre

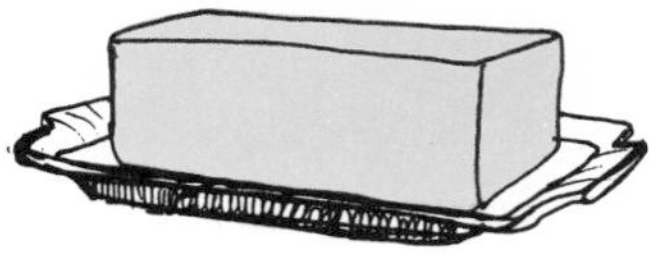

____

Répondez aux questions aloud.

Où est la bière? . . . . **La bière est dans le réfrigérateur.** *(ray-free-zhay-rah-tuhr)*

(luh)
Où est le lait? **Où est le vin?** **Où est le beurre?**

- ☐ **le lac** *(lack)* . . . . lake ______________________
- ☐ **le langage** *(lah$^{(n)}$-gahzh)* . . . . language ______________________
- ☐ **la leçon** *(lay-soh$^{(n)}$)* . . . . lesson ______________________
- ☐ **la lecture** *(lek-tewr)* . . . . reading ______________________
- ☐ **la liberté** *(lee-bear-tay)* . . . . liberty ______________________

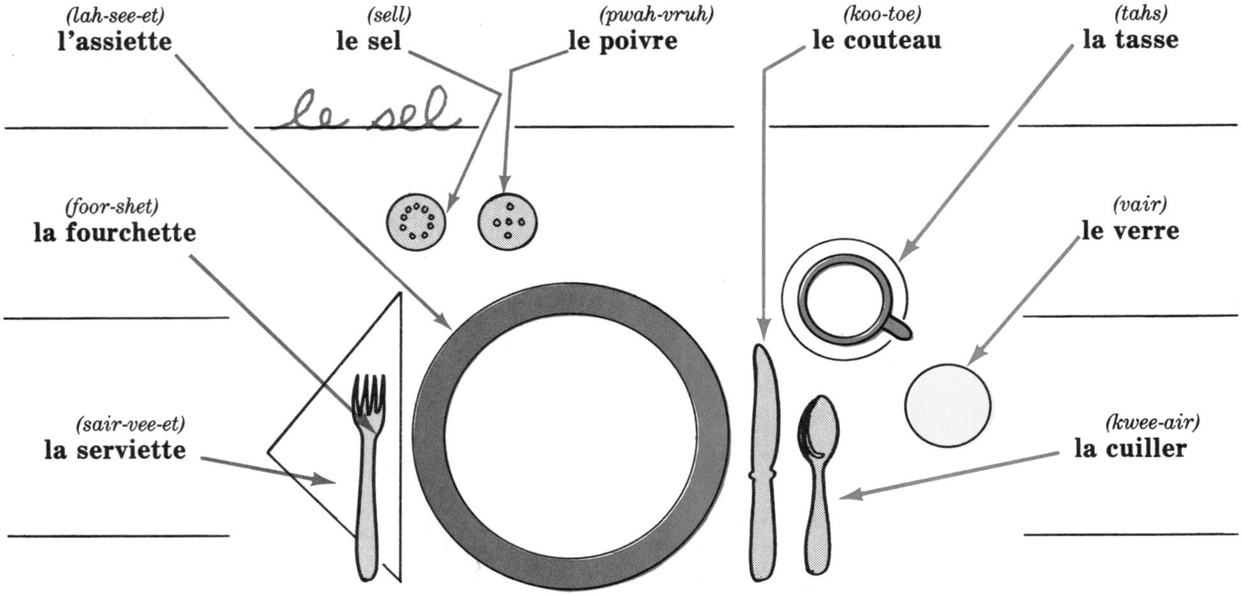

(plah-kar)
le placard

(pa(n))
le pain

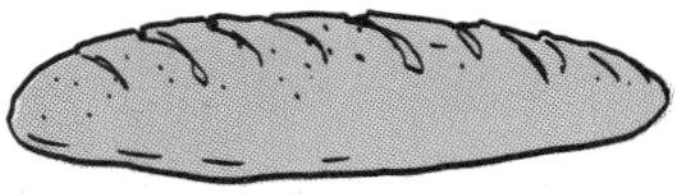

(tay)
le thé

(kah-fay)
le café

_______ _______ le thé _______

Où est le pain? Le pain est dans le placard. Où est le thé? Où est le café? Où est le sel? Où est le poivre? Maintenant ouvrez (oo-vray) (open) your **livre** to the **page avec** the labels **et** remove the next **dix-neuf** labels **et** proceed to label all these **choses** in your **maison.** Do not forget to use every opportunity to say these **mots** out loud. **C'est** (say) **très important!** (a(n)-por-tah(n))

☐ **le lieu** *(lee-uh)*	place	_______
☐ **la ligne** *(leen-yuh)*	line	_______
☐ **la limonade** *(lee-mow-nod)*	lemonade	_______
☐ **le logement** *(lozh-mah(n))*	lodging	_______
☐ **Londres** *(loh(n)-druh)*	London	_______

(lay-gleez) **L'église** (church)

En France, there is not the wide variety of *(ruh-lee-zhee-oh(n))* **religions** (religions) that *(new)* **nous** (we) *(zah-voh(n))* **avons** (have) **ici en Amérique.**

A person's *(ruh-lee-zhee-oh(n))* **religion est** *(zhay-nay-rahl-mah(n))* **généralement** (generally) one of the following.

1. *(kah-toe-leek)* **catholique** (Catholic) catholique
2. *(pro-teh-stah(n))* **protestant** (Protestant) ____________________
3. *(zhew-eef)* **juif** (Jewish) ____________________
4. *(mew-zewl-mah(n))* **musulman** (Moslem) ____________________

Voilà une *(kah-tay-drahl)* **cathédrale** (cathedral) **en France.** →

Est-ce une cathédrale catholique ou *(pro-teh-stah(n)t)** **protestante? Est-ce une nouvelle cathédrale? Non,** *(say)* **c'est une** *(vee-ay)* **vieille** (old) **cathédrale.** You will see *(boh-koo)* **beaucoup** (many) **de** *(bell)* **belles** (beautiful) **cathédrales** like this during your holiday **en France.**

Maintenant let's learn how to say "I am" **en français:** I am = *(zhuh)* **je** *(swee)* **suis** ____________________

Practice saying **"je suis" avec** the following **mots. Maintenant** write each sentence for more practice.

Je suis catholique. ____________________ **Je suis protestant.** ____________________

Je suis juif. Je suis juif. **Je suis américain.** ____________________

Je suis en *(uh-rope)* **Europe.** ____________________ **Je suis en France.** ____________________

*To make an adjective feminine **en français,** all you usually need to do is to add an "e." This will sometimes vary the pronunciation slightly.

☐ **le magasin** *(ma-gah-za(n))*	store	____________
☐ **le magazine** *(ma-gah-zeen)*	magazine	____________
☐ **magnifique** *(mahn-ee-feek)*	magnificent	____________
☐ **le marchand** *(mar-shah(n))*	merchant	____________
☐ **le mécanicien** *(may-kah-nee-see-a(n))*	mechanic	____________

(dah$^{(n)}$)
Je suis dans l'église. ____________ **Je suis dans la cuisine.** ____________
in

Je suis la mère. Je suis la mère. **Je suis le père.** ____________

Je suis dans l'hôtel. ____________ **Je suis dans le restaurant.** ____________

(fah-tee-gay)
Je suis fatigué. ____________ **Je suis à côté de l'église.** ____________

Maintenant identify all **les personnes** *(pear-sohn)* (people) **dans le tableau** below. On the **lignes**, *(leen-yuh)* (lines) write **le mot correct en français** for the **personne** corresponding to **le nombre sous l'image.**

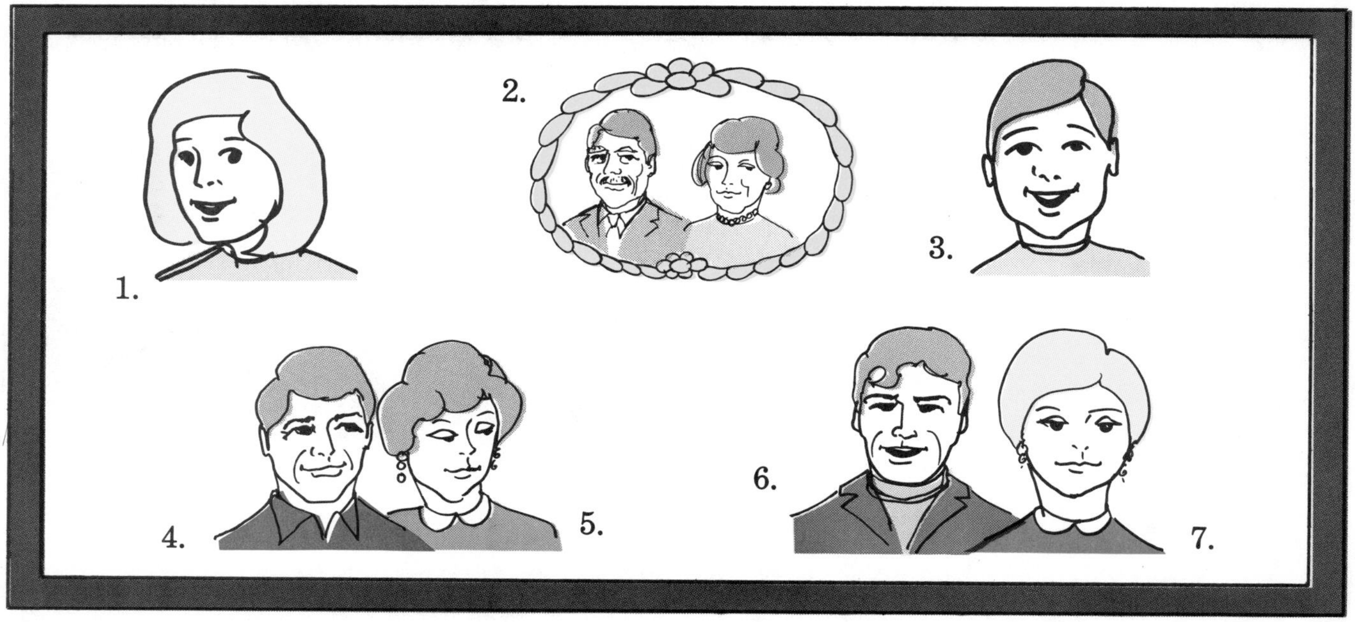

1. ____________ 2. ____________

3. ____________ 4. ____________

5. la tante 6. ____________

7. ____________

Don't be afraid of all of the extra hyphens, apostrophes, accents and uncommon squiggles in French. Concentrate on your easy pronunciation guide and, remember - practice, practice, practice.

est-ce = *(ess)* — is it
qu'est-ce que c'est = *(kess-kuh-say)* — what is that?
s'appelle = *(sah-pel)* — is called

☐ **le marché** *(mar-shay)*	market	____________
— **bon marché** *(boh$^{(n)}$ mar-shay)*	cheap	____________
☐ **le mariage** *(mar-ee-ahzh)*	marriage, wedding	____________
☐ **le médicament** *(may-dee-kah-mah$^{(n)}$)*	medicine	____________
☐ **la mer** *(mare)*	sea	____________

(ah-pruh-nay) Apprenez! learn

(voo) **Vous** (you) have already used the verbs *(ah-vwahr)* **avoir** and *(voo-dray)* **voudrais,** *(koo-tay)* **coûter** (to cost), *(ah-ree-vay)* **arriver**, *(ah^(n)-tray)* **entrer**, *(vuh-neer)* **venir**, *(ray-poh^(n)-druh)* **répondre**, *(ray-pay-tay)* **répéter**, *(ay)* **est**, **sont** and *(swee)* **suis.** Although you might be able to "get by" **avec** these *(vairb)* **verbes,** let's assume you want to do *(mee-yuh)* **mieux** (better) than that. First, a quick review.

How do you say **"I"** **en français?** je How do you say **"we"** **en français?** ______

Compare these **deux** charts very carefully **et** *(ah-pruh-nay)* **apprenez** (learn) these **sept mots** on the right.

I	=	*(zhuh)* **je**
he/it	=	*(eel)* **il**
she/it	=	*(el)* **elle**

we	=	*(new)* **nous**
you	=	*(voo)* **vous**
they	=	*(eel)* **ils** (masculine)
they	=	*(el)* **elles** (feminine)

Maintenant draw *(leen-yuh)* **lignes** *(ah^(n)-truh)* **entre** (between) the matching **mots anglais et mots français** below to see if you can keep these **mots** straight in your mind.

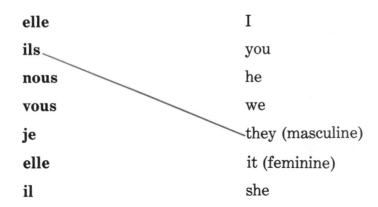

elle	I
ils	you
nous	he
vous	we
je	they (masculine)
elle	it (feminine)
il	she

Maintenant close **le livre et** write out both columns of the above practice on *(ewn)* **une** *(fuh-yuh)* **feuille de** *(pah-pee-ay)* **papier.** How did **vous** do? *(bee-ya^(n))* **Bien** (well) **ou** *(mahl)* **mal?** (poorly) *(pah)* **Pas bien,** (not too well) **pas mal?** (not too bad) **Maintenant** that *(voo)* **vous** know these **mots,** you will soon be able to say almost anything *(kuh)* **que** (that) **vous** *(day-zee-ray)* **désirez** (desire) by using a type of "plug-in" formula.

☐ **le métropolitain** *(may-tro-poh-lee-ta^(n))* . . .	subway (metro!)	______
☐ **la minute** *(mee-newt)*	minute	______
— **la minuterie** *(mee-new-tuh-ree)*.	automatic light switch	______
☐ **la mode** *(mode)*	fashion	______
— **à la mode**	fashionable	______

To demonstrate, here are *(seez)* **six exemples** of very practical **et** important **verbes français.** These are **verbes** whose basic form ends in **"er."** Write **les verbes** in the blanks below **after vous** have practiced them out loud many times.

(par-lay) **parler** = to speak

(reh-stay) **rester** = to remain/stay

(ah-bee-tay) **habiter** = to live/reside

______ rester ______ ______

(ko-mah(n)-day) **commander** = to order

(ah-shuh-tay) **acheter** = to buy

(saw-puh-lay) **s'appeler** = to be called

______ ______ ______

Study the following verb patterns **avec attention.**

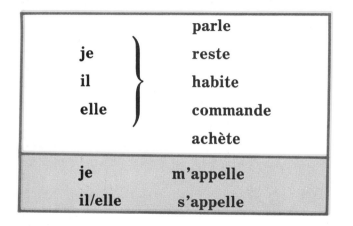

je / il / elle	**parle**
	reste
	habite
	commande
	achète
je	**m'appelle**
il/elle	**s'appelle**

nous	**parlons**
	restons
	habitons
	commandons
	achetons
nous	**nous appelons**

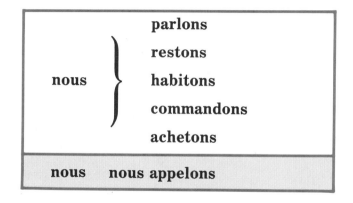

Note:
- With **je, il,** or **elle** you drop the final "r" from the basic verb form.
- With **nous** you drop the final "er" of the basic verb form and substitute "ons" in its place. **Exemple: nous** (we) *(par-loh(n))* **parlons.** (speak)
- **S'appeler** varies but not too much. It is a very important verb so take a few extra minutes to learn it.

Some **verbes en français** will not conform to rules quite as easily as these **verbes** do. But don't worry . . . you will be perfectly understood whether you say **"parle"** or **"parlons."** **Les Français** will be delighted that you have taken the time to learn their language.

- ☐ **le monde** *(mohnd)* . . . . world ______
- — **tout le monde** *(too luh mohnd)* . . . . everyone ______
- ☐ **la montagne** *(moh(n)-tahn-yuh)* . . . . mountain ______
- ☐ **le musée** *(mew-zay)* . . . . museum ______
- ☐ **la musique** *(mew-zeek)* . . . . music ______

Note: • With **vous** you drop the final "r" from the basic verb form and add "z."

Exemple: vous (you) **parlez** *(par-lay)* (speak)**.** This form is pronounced exactly as the basic verb form!

• With **ils** or **elles** you drop the final "r" and add "nt."

Important! Concentrate on the **similarités** *(see-mee-lar-ee-tay)* of pronunciation **en français** rather than on the spelling. It's really much easier than it looks.

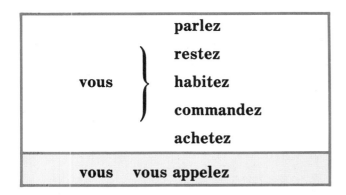

vous	**parlez** **restez** **habitez** **commandez** **achetez**
vous	**vous appelez**

ils **elles**	**parlent** **restent** **habitent** **commandent** **achètent**
ils/elles	**s'appellent**

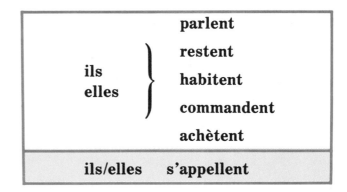

Here are a few hints for mixing and matching verbs and their subjects.

-ons ⟶ **nous** ex. **nous parlons**

-ez ⟶ **vous** ex. **vous parlez**

-ent ⟶ **ils** ex. **ils parlent**
elles ex. **elles parlent**

Maintenant, read through the entire verb form aloud several times before writing out each form in its blank. Notice in the first pattern, how despite the difference in spelling, the verbs are pronounced the same (*).

parler

Je* parle/ **français.**

Il* / **Elle** parle/ **français.**

Nous parlons/ **français.**

Vous parlez/ **anglais.**

Ils* / **Elles** parlent/ **anglais.**

rester

Je* reste/ **en France.**

Il* / **Elle** reste/ **en Amérique.**

Nous restons/ **dans un hôtel.**

Vous restez/ **en Europe.**

Ils* / **Elles** restent/ **en Belgique.**

☐ **la nation** *(nah-see-oh(n))*	nation	________
☐ **la nature** *(nah-tewr)*	nature	________
☐ **naturel** *(nah-tew-rel)*	natural	________
— **au naturel** *(oh nah-tew-rel)*	plain, simple	________
☐ **la nécessité** *(nay-say-see-tay)*	necessity	________

habiter

J' habite/ ______________ en France.

Il
Elle ______________ en Amérique.

Nous ______________ en Italie.

Vous ______________ en Europe.

Ils
Elles ______________ en Chine.

s'appeler

Je ______________ Jeanne Guégan.

Il
Elle ______________ Mitou.

Nous ______________ Smith.

Vous ______________ Thierry Huck.

Ils
Elles ______________ Roquefort.

acheter

J' achète/ ______________ un livre.

Il
Elle ______________ une salade.

Nous ______________ une auto.

Vous ______________ une horloge.

Ils
Elles ______________ une lampe.

commander

Je ______________ un verre d'eau.

Il
Elle ______________ un verre de vin.

Nous ______________ une tasse de thé.

Vous ______________ une tasse de café.

Ils
Elles ______________ un verre de lait.

Remember these **verbes?**

(vuh-neer) **venir** = to come — venir ______________

(ah-lay) **aller** = to go ______________

(ah-prah(n)-druh) **apprendre** = to learn ______________

(voo-dray) **voudrais** = would like ______________

(ah-vwahr) **avoir** = to have ______________

avoir (to have) **besoin** *(buh-zwa(n))* (need) **de** (of) = to need ______________

Here we have **six,** already familiar **verbes** whose following forms might seem a bit erratic after our last group. DON'T PANIC or give up. Read them out loud, practice them, think of their **similarités,** write them out and then try to use them in sentences of your own.

☐ **neuf** *(nuf)*	new	______________
— **Le Pont Neuf à Paris** *(poh(n) nuf)*	new bridge in Paris (1604)	______________
☐ **Noël** *(no-el)*	Christmas	______________
☐ **le nord** *(nor)*	north	______________
☐ **Notre-Dame de Paris** *(no-truh dahm)*	Our Lady (cathedral)	______________

Think of how hard it would be to speak **en anglais** with no verbs — it's the same **en français.**

venir

Je viens/ ______ **de l'Amérique.**

Il / Elle vient/ ______ **de la Belgique.**

Nous venons/ ______ **du Canada.**

Vous venez/ ______ **de New York.**

Ils / Elles viennent/ ______ **de la Suisse.**

apprendre

J' apprends/ ______ **le français.**

Il / Elle apprend/ ______ **l'anglais.**

Nous apprenons/ ______ **la géometrie.**

Vous apprenez/ ______ **l'allemand.**

Ils / Elles apprennent/ ______ **l'espagnol.**

avoir

J' ai/ ______ **cinq francs.**

Il / Elle a/ ______ **six francs.**

Nous avons/ ______ **dix francs.**

Vous avez/ ______ **deux francs.**

Ils / Elles ont/ ______ **trois francs.**

aller

Je vais/ ______ **en France.**

Il / Elle va/ ______ **en Italie.**

Nous allons/ ______ **en Angleterre.**

Vous allez/ ______ **en Europe.**

Ils / Elles vont/ ______ **en Chine.**

voudrais / voudrions

Je voudrais/ ______ **un verre de vin.**

Il / Elle voudrait/ ______ **un verre de vin rouge.**

Nous voudrions ______ **un verre de vin blanc.**

Vous voudriez/ ______ **un verre de lait.**

Ils / Elles voudraient/ ______ **un verre de bière.**

avoir besoin de

J' ai besoin ______ **d'un verre de vin.**

Il / Elle ______ **d'un verre de vin rouge.**

Nous ______ **d'un verre de vin blanc.**

Vous ______ **d'un verre de lait.**

Ils / Elles ______ **d'un verre de bière.**

- ☐ **l'objet** *(lobe-zhay)* .... object ______
- ☐ **obligatoire** *(oh-blee-gah-twahr)* .... compulsory ______
- ☐ **l'observation** *(lobe-sair-vah-see-oh(n))* .... observation ______
- ☐ **l'occupation** *(low-kew-pah-see-oh(n))* ..... profession, occupation ______
- ☐ **l'odeur** *(low-dur)* .... smell, odor ______

Maintenant take a deep breath. See if **vous** can fill in the blanks below. **Les réponses correctes sont** at the bottom of **la page.**

1. I speak French. ______________________
2. He comes from America. ______________________
3. We learn French. ______________________
4. They (masc.) have 10 francs. ______________________
5. She would like a glass of water. ______________________
6. We need a room. **(chambre)** Nous avons besoin d'une chambre.
7. My name is Paul Smith. ______________________
8. I live in America. ______________________
9. You are buying a book. ______________________
10. He orders a beer. ______________________

In the following Steps, **vous** will be introduced to more **et** more **verbes et** should drill them in exactly the same way as **vous** did in this section. Look up **les nouveaux** *(noo-voh)* **mots** in your **dictionnaire** *(deek-see-oh-nair)* dictionary **et** make up your own sentences using the same type of pattern. **Try** out your **nouveaux mots** for that's how you make them yours to use on your holiday. Remember, the more **vous** practice **maintenant,** the more enjoyable your trip will be.

Bonne chance!

Be sure to check off your free **mots** in the box provided as **vous apprenez** each one.

RÉPONSES

1. **Je parle français.**
2. **Il vient de l'Amérique.**
3. **Nous apprenons le français.**
4. **Ils ont dix francs.**
5. **Elle voudrait un verre d'eau.**
6. **Nous avons besoin d'une chambre.**
7. **Je m'appelle Paul Smith.**
8. **J'habite en Amérique.**
9. **Vous achetez un livre.**
10. **Il commande une bière.**

L'Heure
(luhr)
hour

Vous know how to tell **les** (lay) **jours** (days) **de la semaine** (week) **et les mois de l'année** (year), so **maintenant** let's learn to tell time. As a **voyageur** (vwhy-ah-zhur) (traveler) **en France, vous** need to be able to tell time for **réservations, rendez-vous et trains. Voilà les** "basics."

What time is it?	=	**Quelle** (kel) **heure** (uhr) **est-il?** (ay-teel) ______

half past	=	**et demie** (duh-mee) ______
less	=	**moins** (mwa(n)) ~~moins~~
midnight	=	**minuit** (mee-nwee) ______
noon	=	**midi** (mee-dee) ______

Il est cinq heures.

Il est quatre heures et demie.

Il est trois heures.

Il est deux heures et demie.

Il est midi/minuit.

Il est huit heures vingt.

Il est sept heures quarante. **OU** **Il est huit heures moins vingt.**

Maintenant fill in the blanks according to **l'heure** (luhr) (hour) indicated **sur** (on) **l'horloge** (clock).

Il (eel) **est** (ay) ______________.

Il est ______________.

Il est ______________.

Il est ______________.

Il est ______________.

Il est quatre heures.

Il est ______________.

Il est ______________.

RÉPONSES

Il est dix heures dix.
Il est deux heures vingt.
Il est sept heures et demie.
Il est six heures dix.

Il est une heure et demie.
Il est quatre heures.
Il est midi (ou minuit) vingt.
Il est six heures moins dix.
(Il est cinq heures cinquante.)

Voilà more time-telling **mots** to add to your **mot** power.

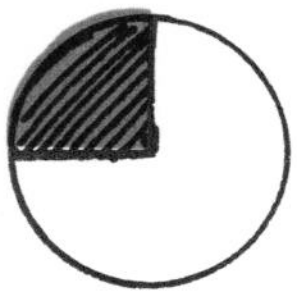

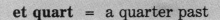

un quart *(kahr)*	=	a quarter
moins le quart	=	a quarter to
et quart	=	a quarter past

Il est deux heures et quart. OU Il est deux heures quinze.

Il est deux heures moins le quart. OU Il est une heure quarante-cinq.

Maintenant, your turn.

Il est trois heures et quart.

Il est ______________________.

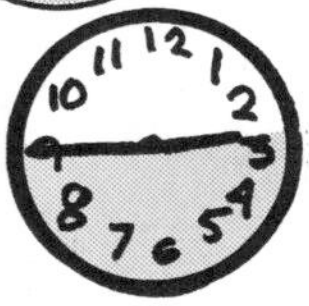

Il est ______________________.

Il est ______________________.

Les nombres — see how **importants** they have become! **Maintenant, répondez aux questions suivantes** *(swee-vah$^{(n)}$t)* following based on **les horloges** below.

Quelle heure est-il?

1 

2 

3 

4 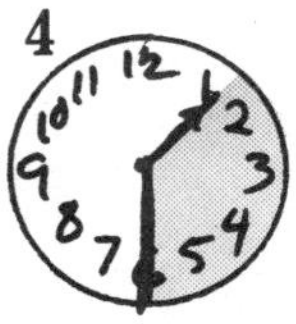

5 

6 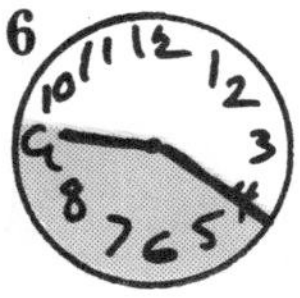

7 

1. ______________________
2. Il est sept heures et demie.
3. ______________________
4. ______________________
5. ______________________
6. ______________________
7. ______________________

RÉPONSES

1. **Il est six heures.**
2. **Il est sept heures et demie.**
3. **Il est huit heures.**
4. **Il est une heure et demie.**
5. **Il est midi (ou minuit) et quart.** **Il est midi (ou minuit) quinze.**
6. **Il est neuf heures vingt.**
7. **Il est six heures moins le quart.** **Il est cinq heures quarante-cinq.**

When **vous** answer a **"Quand"** question, say **"à"** (at) before you give the time.

Quand le train arrive-t-il? à six heures.

Maintenant, répondez aux questions suivantes *(swee-vah^(n)t)* based on **les horloges** below. Be sure to practice saying each question out loud several times.

Quand *(kah^(n))* **le concert** *(koh^(n)-sair)* **commence-t-il?** *(ko-mah^(n)s-teel)* (begins ... it) ________________.

Quand le film commence-t-il? ________________.

Quand l'autobus jaune arrive-t-il? ________________.

Quand le taxi arrive-t-il? ________________.

Quand le restaurant est-il ouvert? *(oo-vair)* (open) à cinq heures.

Quand le restaurant est-il fermé? *(fair-may)* (closed) ________________.

A huit heures du (in the) **matin on** *(oh^(n))* (one) **dit:** *(dee)* (says)

"Bonjour, Madame *(mah-dahm)* (Mrs.) **Dupont."**

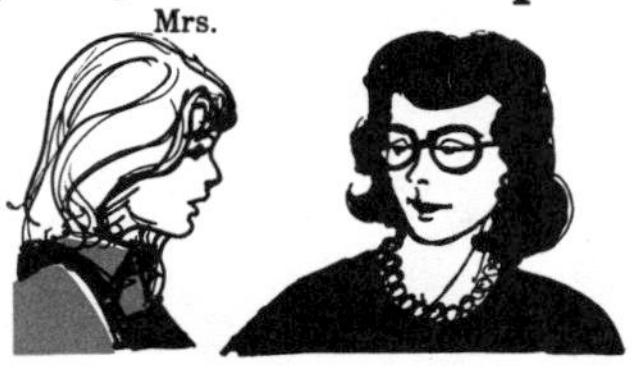

A huit heures du (in the) **soir on dit:**

"Bonsoir, Mademoiselle *(mad-mwah-zel)* (Miss) **Vartan."**

A une heure de l'après-midi on dit:

"Bonjour, Monsieur *(muh-see-uh)* (Mr.) **Monet."**

A dix heures du soir on dit:

"Bonne nuit."

☐ **occupé** *(oh-kew-pay)*	busy, occupied	________
— une ligne occupée	engaged telephone line	________
☐ **officiel** *(oh-fee-see-el)*	official	________
☐ **l'Orient** *(lor-ee-ah^(n))*	Orient	________
☐ **l'orchestre** *(lor-kess-truh)*	orchestra	________

Remember:

What time is it? = **Quelle heure est-il?**	When/at what time? = **Quand? A quelle heure?**

Can **vous** pronounce **et** understand **le**

(pah-rah-grahf) *(swee-vah(n))*
paragraphe suivant?
paragraph

Le train de Lyon arrive à 15:15. Il est maintenant 15:20. Le train est *(ah(n))(ruh-tar)* **en retard** (late). **Le train arrive aujourd'hui à 17:15. Demain le train arrive** *(ah(n)-kor)* **encore** (again) **à 15:15.**

Voilà more practice exercises. **Répondez aux questions** based on **l'heure** given.

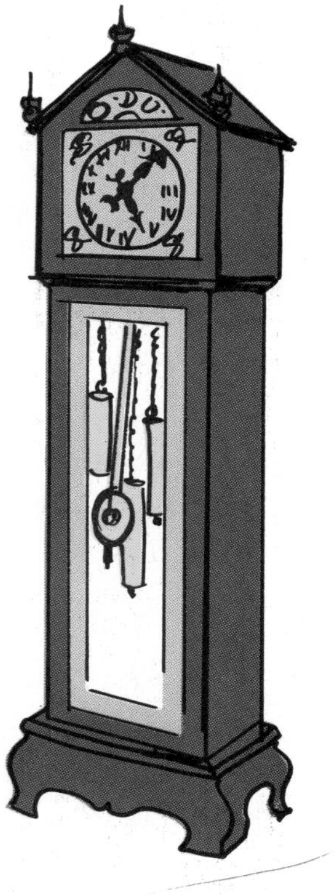

Quelle heure est-il?

1. (10:30) ______________________________
2. (6:30) ______________________________
3. (2:15) Il est deux heures et quart.
4. (11:40) ______________________________
5. (12:18) ______________________________
6. (7:20) ______________________________
7. (3:10) ______________________________
8. (4:05) ______________________________
9. (5:35) ______________________________
10. (11:50) ______________________________

☐ **l'omelette** *(low-muh-let)* . . . . omelette ____________
☐ **on** *(oh(n))* . . . . one, people, they, we, etc. ____________
— **On fait ça.** *(oh(n) fay sah)* . . . . One does that. ____________
— **On dit que . . .** *(oh(n) dee kuh)* . . . . They say that . . . ____________
☐ **l'optimiste** *(lowp-tee-meest)* . . . . optimist ____________

Voilà a quick quiz. Fill in the blanks **avec les nombres corrects. Les réponses sont en** *(ah(n))* **bas** *(bah)* (below).

1. **Une minute a** (has) ______ (?) **secondes.**
2. **Une heure a** ______ (?) **minutes.**
3. **Un jour a** ______ (?) **heures.**
4. **Une semaine a** ______ (?) **jours.**
5. **Un mois a** trente (?) **jours.**
6. **Un an** *(ah(n))* (year) **a** ______ (?) **mois.**
7. **Un an a** ______ (?) **semaines.**
8. **Un an a** ______ (?) **jours.**

Voilà a sample page from **un horaire** *(or-air)* (timetable) **de SNCF** *(ess-n-say-ef)* — the French national railroad. **Un TEE et un rapide (RAP) sont très rapides** *(rah-peed)* (fast), **un express (EXP) est rapide, et un omnibus (OMN) est lent** *(lah(n))* (slow).

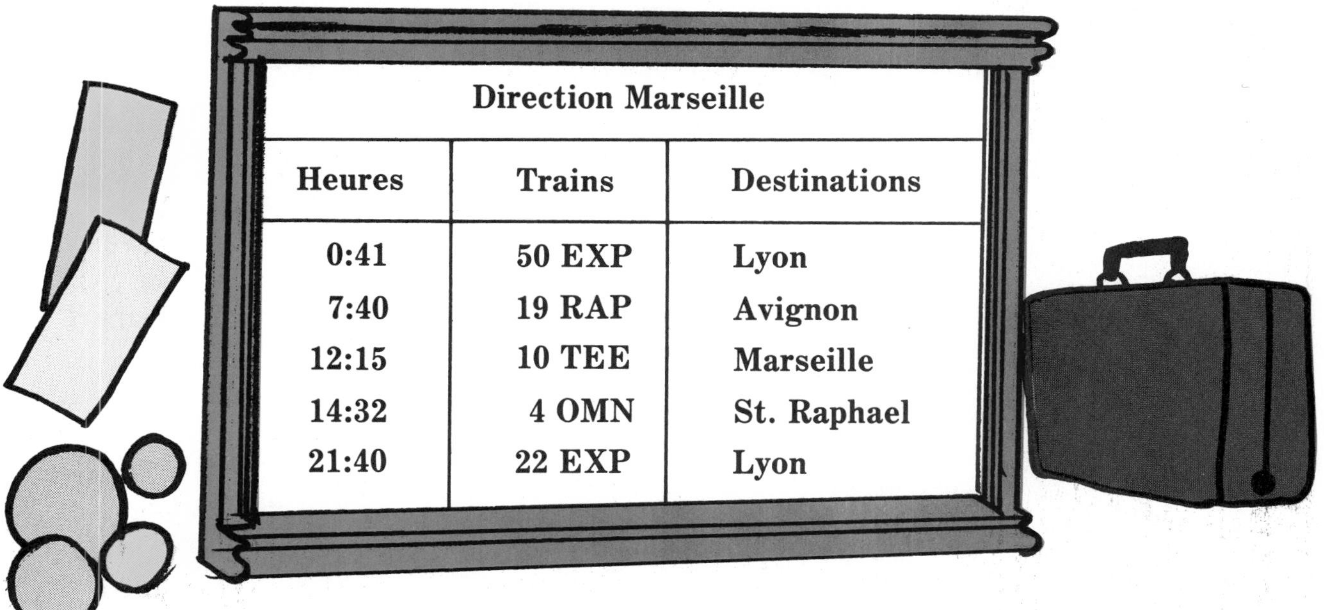

Direction Marseille		
Heures	**Trains**	**Destinations**
0:41	50 EXP	Lyon
7:40	19 RAP	Avignon
12:15	10 TEE	Marseille
14:32	4 OMN	St. Raphael
21:40	22 EXP	Lyon

RÉPONSES

1. soixante
2. soixante
3. vingt-quatre
4. sept
5. trente
6. douze
7. cinquante-deux
8. trois cent soixante-cinq

Voilà trois nouveaux verbes **pour** *(poor)* for Step 12.

dire *(deer)* = to say	**manger** *(mah$^{(n)}$-zhay)* = to eat	**boire** *(bwahr)* = to drink
dire	____________	____________

dire

Je dis/ ____________ "**Bonjour.**"

Il / Elle dit/ ____________ "**Salut.**"

Nous disons/ ____________ "**Non.**" *(noh$^{(n)}$)* no

Vous dites/ ____________ "**Oui.**" *(wee)* yes

Ils / Elles ne disent/ ____________ **rien.** *(ree-a$^{(n)}$)* nothing

manger

Je mange/ ____________ **de la soupe.**

Il / Elle mange/ ____________ **un bifteck.**

Nous mangeons/ ____________ **beaucoup.**

Vous ne mangez/ ____________ **rien.** *(ree-a$^{(n)}$)* nothing

Ils / Elles mangent/ ____________ **des escargots.** *(ess-kar-go)* snails

boire

Je bois/ ____________ **du lait.**

Il / Elle boit/ ____________ **du vin blanc.**

Nous buvons/ ____________ **des bières.**

Vous buvez/ ____________ **un verre d'eau.**

Ils / Elles boivent/ ____________ **du thé.**

Remember that "**oi**" as in **le verbe "boire"** sounds like "wah." Practice this sound **avec les mots suivants: bois** *(bwah)*, **boit** *(bwah)*, **trois, soixante, mademoiselle, poivre** (pepper), **bonsoir.**

☐ **ordinaire** *(or-dee-nair)*	ordinary	____________
☐ **organisé** *(or-gah-nee-zay)*	organized	____________
☐ **l'origine** *(loh-ree-zheen)*	origin	____________
— Je suis d'origine américaine	I am of American origin.	____________
☐ **l'ouest** *(loo-west)*	west	____________

(pa(n)) le **pain**	(pah-pee-ay) le **papier**	(sah-voh(n)) le **savon**	(koh(n)-play) le **complet**
(tay) le **thé**	(leh-truh) la **lettre**	(brohs) (ah) (dah(n)) la **brosse à dents**	(krah-vat) la **cravate**
(kah-fay) le **café**	(kart) (pohs-tall) la **carte postale**	(dah(n)-tee-frees) le **dentifrice**	(moo-shwar) le **mouchoir**
(show-ko-lah) le **chocolat**	(ta(n)-bruh-post) le **timbre-poste**	(pen-yuh) le **peigne**	(shuh-meez) la **chemise**
(loh) **l'eau**	(lee-vruh) le **livre**	(mah(n)-toe) le **manteau**	(veh-stoh(n)) le **veston**
(lee) le **lit**	(ruh-vew) la **revue**	(la(n)-pear-may-ah-bluh) **l'imperméable**	(pah(n)-tah-loh(n)) le **pantalon**
(koo-vair-tewr) la **couverture**	(zhoor-nahl) le **journal**	(pah-rah-plew-ee) le **parapluie**	(rohb) la **robe**
(low-ray-yay) **l'oreiller**	(lew-net) les **lunettes**	(gah(n)) les **gants**	(blooz) la **blouse**
(ray-vay) le **réveil**	(tay-lay-vee-zee-oh(n)) la **télévision**	(shah-poh) le **chapeau**	(zhewp) la **jupe**
(lar-mwahr) **l'armoire**	(kor-bay-uh) (ah) (pah-pee-ay) la **corbeille à papier**	(boat) les **bottes**	(shah(n)-dye) le **chandail**
(lah-vah-boh) le **lavabo**	(pass-por) le **passeport**	(show-sewr) les **chaussures**	(soo-tee-a(n)-gorzh) le **soutien-gorge**
(doosh) la **douche**	(bee-ay) le **billet**	(show-set) les **chaussettes**	(koh(n)-bee-nay-zoh(n)) la **combinaison**
(doo-bul-vay-say) le **W.C.**	(vah-leez) la **valise**	(bah) les **bas**	(sleep) le **slip**
(mir-wahr) le **miroir**	(sack) (ah) (ma(n)) le **sac à main**	(pee-zhah-mah) le **pyjama**	(tree-ko) (duh) (poh) le **tricot de peau**
(gah(n)) (duh) (twah-let) le **gant de toilette**	(port-fuh-yuh) le **portefeuille**	(shuh-meez) (duh) (nwee) la **chemise de nuit**	(bun) (ah-pay-tee) **bon appétit**
(sair-vee-et) la **serviette**	(lar-zhah(n)) **l'argent**	(rohb) (duh) (shah(n)-bruh) la **robe de chambre**	(oh-kew-pay) **occupé**
(puh-teet) (sair-vee-et) la **petite serviette**	(lah-pah-ray) (photo) **l'appareil photo**	(pah(n)-too-fluh) les **pantoufles**	(ek-skew-zay-mwah) **excusez-moi**
(sair-vee-et) (duh) (ba(n)) la **serviette de bain**	(peh-lee-kewl) la **pellicule**	(zhuh) (swee) (zah-may-ree-ka(n)) **Je suis américain.**	
(kray-oh(n)) le **crayon**	(my-oh) le **maillot**	(zhuh) (voo-dray) (zah-prah(n)-druh) (luh) (frah(n)-say) **Je voudrais apprendre le français**	
(stee-low) le **stylo**	(sah(n)-dahl) les **sandales**	(zhuh) (mah-pel) **Je m'appelle ________________.**	

PLUS . . .

Your book includes a number of other innovative features. At the back of the book, you'll find seven pages of flash cards. Cut them out and flip through them at least once a day.

On pages 112 and 113, you'll find a beverage guide and a menu guide. Don't wait until your trip to use them. Clip out the menu guide and use it tonight at the dinner table. And use the beverage guide to practice ordering your favorite drinks.

By using the special features in this book, you will be speaking French before you know it.

(ah-mew-zay-voo)
Amusez-vous!
have fun

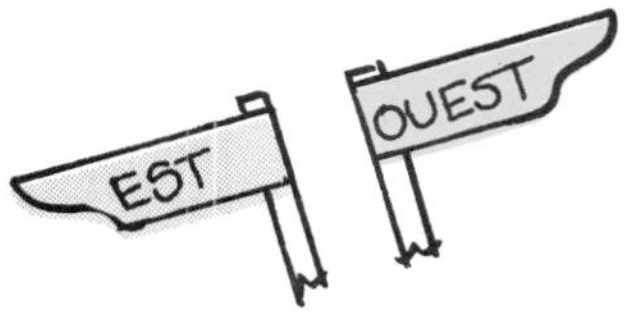

(nor) (sood) (est) (west)
Nord - sud, est - ouest
north south east west

If **vous** are looking at **une** **carte** *(kart)* [map] **et vous** see **les mots suivants,** it should not be too **difficile** *(dee-fee-seal)* [difficult] to figure out what **ils** *(eel)* [they] mean. Take an educated guess. **Les réponses sont en bas.** *(ahⁿ)(bah)*

(lah-may-reek) (dew) (nor) **l'Amérique du nord**	*(lah-may-reek) (dew) (sood)* **l'Amérique du sud**	*(lahl-mahn-yuh) (duh) (loo-west)* **l'Allemagne de l'ouest**
(mare) **la Mer du nord**	*(lah-freek)* **l'Afrique du sud**	*(lahl-mahn-yuh) (lest)* **l'Allemagne de l'est**
(leer-lahnd) **l'Irelande du nord**	*(kah-row-leen)* **la Caroline du sud**	*(tay-ree-twahr) (dew) (nor-west)* **les Territoires du nord-ouest**
(dah-koh-tah) **le Dakota du nord**	*(pole)* **le Pôle sud**	*(pole)* **le Pôle nord**

Les mots français pour north, south, east **et** west **sont** easy to recognize due to their **similarités** to **anglais.** So . . .

(nor) **le nord**	=	the north	____________	*(dew)* **du nord**	=	northern	____________
(sood) **le sud**	=	the south	le sud	**du sud**	=	southern	____________
(lest) **l'est**	=	the east	____________	*(duh)* **de l'est**	=	eastern	de l'est
(loo-west) **l'ouest**	=	the west	____________	**de l'ouest**	=	western	____________

These **mots sont très importants.** Learn them **aujourd'hui.** But what about more basic **directions** *(dee-rek-see-ohⁿ)* [directions] such as "left," "right," **et** "straight ahead"? Let's learn these **mots.**

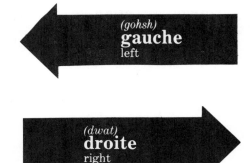

(gohsh) **gauche** left

(dwat) **droite** right

straight ahead	=	*(too) (dwah)* **tout droit**
to the left	=	*(ah)(gohsh)* **à gauche**
to the right	=	*(ah)(dwat)* **à droite**

RÉPONSES

North America	South America	West Germany
North Sea	South Africa	East Germany
Northern Ireland	South Carolina	Northwest Territories
North Dakota	South Pole	North Pole

Just as **en anglais,** these **trois mots** go a long way.

(sill) (voo) (play) **s'il vous plaît**	= please	
(mare-see) **merci**	= thank you	merci, merci, merci
(par-doh$^{(n)}$) **pardon**	= excuse me	
(ek-skew-zay-mwah) **excusez-moi**	= excuse me	

Voilà deux conversations *(koh$^{(n)}$vair-sah-see-oh$^{(n)}$)* **typiques** *(tee-peek)* [typical] **pour** someone who is trying to find something.

Jean-Paul: **Excusez-moi, mais** *(may)* [but] **où est l'Hôtel Cézanne?**

Claude: **Continuez** *(koh$^{(n)}$-tee-new-ay)* [continue] **tout droit, puis tournez** *(toor-nay)* [turn] **à gauche à la deuxième** [second] **rue** *(rew)* [street] **et l'Hôtel est juste** *(zhoost)* [just] **à droite.**

Jean-Paul: **Pardon, Monsieur. Où est le Musée français?**

Claude: **Tournez à droite ici, continuez tout droit approximativement cent mètres et puis tournez à gauche et le musée est au coin** *(oh) (kwa$^{(n)}$)* [on the corner]**.**

Are you lost? There is no need to be lost if **vous** *(voo)* **avez** *(zah-vay)* [have] learned the basic **mots de direction** *(dee-rek-see-oh$^{(n)}$)***.** Do not try to memorize these **conversations** because you will never be looking for precisely these places. One day you might need to ask for **directions** to **"Maxim's" ou "le Louvre" ou "l'Hôtel Maurice."** Learn the key **mots de direction et** be sure **vous** can find your **destination** *(day-stee-nah-see-oh$^{(n)}$)* [destination]**.**

What if the person responding to your **question** answers too quickly for you to understand the entire reply? If so, ask again, saying,

☐ **la paire** *(pair)*	pair	
☐ **le pantalon** *(pah$^{(n)}$-tah-loh$^{(n)}$)*	pair of trousers	
☐ **le Pape** *(pahp)*	Pope	
☐ **parfait** *(par-fay)*	perfect	
— **C'est parfait**	That's fine.	

Excusez-moi. Je suis américain et je parle seulement (suhl-mah(n)) [only] un [a] peu (puh) [little] de français. Parlez plus (plew) [more] lentement (lah(n)t-mah(n)) [slowly], s'il vous plaît, et répétez votre (voh-truh) [your] réponse. Merci beaucoup (boh-koo).

Maintenant quand [when] the directions are repeated, **vous** will be able to understand if **vous** (voo) **avez** (zah-vay) [have] learned the key **mots** for directions. Quiz yourself by filling in the blanks **en bas avec les mots corrects en français.**

Jean-Louis: **Pardon, Mademoiselle. Où est le restaurant "Le Cygne" (seen-yuh) [swan]?**

Chantal: **D'ici** (dee-see) [from here]**, continuez** ______________ (straight ahead)**, puis à la troisième** [third] rue (street) **tournez** à ______ (right). **Il y a** [there is] **une église. Juste après** ______________ (the church) ______________ (turn) **encore** (ah(n)-kor) [again] ______________ (right) **et le restaurant "Le Cygne" est** ______________ (on the left), au coin (on the corner).

Bonne chance.

Voilà quatre nouveaux verbes.

attendre (ah-tah(n)-druh)	= to wait for	attendre, attendre,
comprendre (koh(n)-prah(n)-druh)	= to understand	______________
vendre (vah(n)-druh)	= to sell	______________
répéter (ray-pay-tay)	= to repeat	______________

- ☐ **le parc** *(park)* .... park ______________
- ☐ **le parfum** *(par-fuh(n))* .... perfume ______________
- **— la parfumerie** *(par-few-muh-ree)* ..... perfumery ______________
- ☐ **le parking** *(par-keeng)* .... parking lot ______________
- ☐ **le passeport** *(pass-por)* .... passport ______________

As always, say each sentence out loud. **Say each and every mot carefully**, pronouncing each French sound as well as **vous** can.

attendre

J' attends/ ______ le train.

Il / Elle attend/ ______ l'autobus.

Nous attendons/ ______ le taxi.

Vous ______ devant l'hôtel.

Ils / Elles ______ Jacques.

comprendre

Je comprends/ ______ l'anglais.

Il / Elle ______ le français.

Nous comprenons/ ______ l'italien.

Vous ______ le menu.

Ils / Elles ______ le russe.

vendre

Je vends/ ______ des fleurs. (some)

Il / Elle vend/ ______ du fruit.

Nous ______ une jaquette.

Vous ______ une banane.

Ils / Elles ______ beaucoup de tickets.

répéter

Je ______ le mot.

Il / Elle ______ la réponse.

Nous ______ les noms.

Vous répétez/ ______ la leçon.

Ils / Elles ______ le verbe.

Maintenant, see if **vous** can translate the following thoughts **en français. Les réponses sont en bas.**

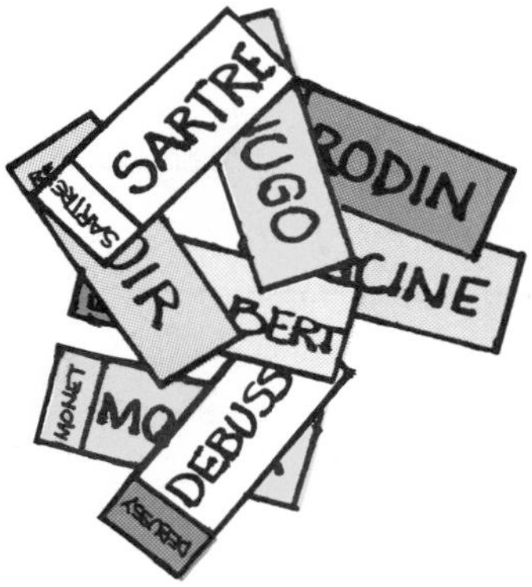

1. She repeats the word. ______
2. You sell many tickets. ______
3. He waits for the taxi. Il attend le taxi.
4. We eat some fruit. ______
5. I speak French. ______
6. I drink a cup of tea. ______

RÉPONSES

1. **Elle répète le mot.**
2. **Vous vendez beaucoup de tickets.**
3. **Il attend le taxi.**
4. **Nous mangeons des fruits.**
5. **Je parle français.**
6. **Je bois une tasse de thé.**

En haut - en bas
(ah(n)) (oh) (bah)
En haut = above; **en bas** = below

Step 14

Before **vous commencez** *(koh-mah(n)-say)* [begin] Step 14, review Step 8. **Maintenant nous apprenons encore** *(ah(n)-kor)* [more] **des mots.**

Voilà une maison *(maze-oh(n))* **en France.**

La chambre *(shah(n)-bruh)* **à coucher** *(koo-shay)* **est en haut.**

La salle *(sahl)* **de bain** *(ba(n))* **est aussi** [also] **en haut.**

Le bureau *(bew-row)* **est en bas.**

Le living-room est aussi en bas.

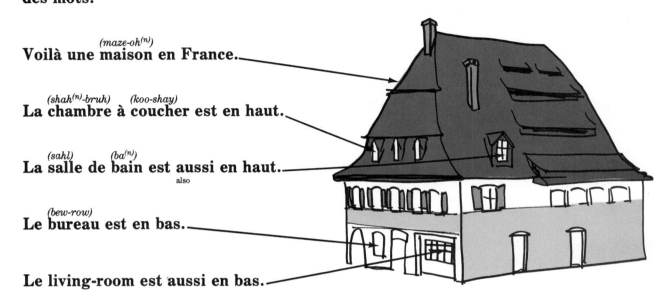

Allez *(ah-lay)* [go] **maintenant dans** your **chambre à coucher et** look around **la pièce** *(pea-ess)*. Let's learn **les noms des** [of the] **choses dans la chambre** just as **nous** *(new)* **avons** *(zah-voh(n))* learned the various parts of **la maison.** Be sure to practice saying **les mots** as you write them in the spaces **en bas.**

Also say out loud the example sentences **sous les images.**

le lit *(lee)*

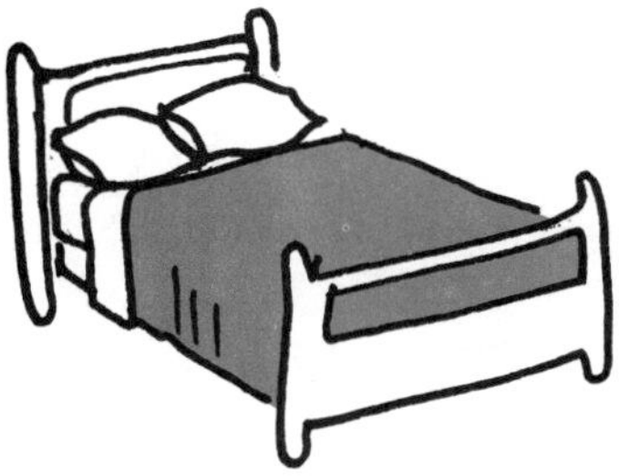

____

J'achète le lit.

la couverture *(koo-vair-tewr)* [blanket]

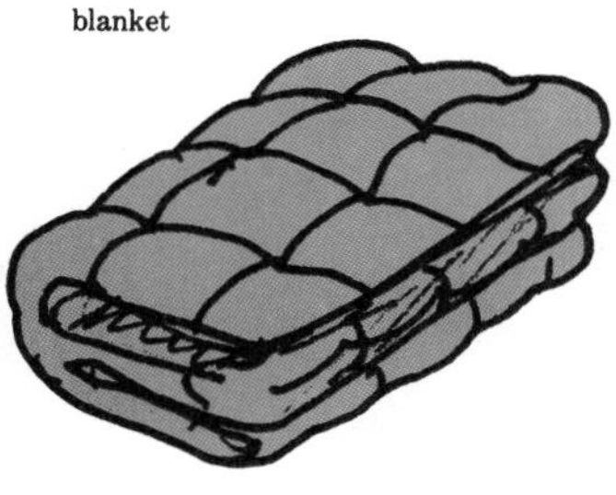

____

J'ai besoin [need] **d'une couverture.**

l'oreiller *(low-ray-yay)* [pillow]

l'oreiller

L'oreiller est très grand.

- ☐ **la pâtisserie** *(pah-tee-suh-ree)* . . . . pastry, pastry shop _______________
- ☐ **le peuple français** *(puh-pluh)* . . . . French people _______________
- ☐ **la pharmacie** *(far-mah-see)* . . . . pharmacy _______________
- ☐ **la photo** *(pho-toh)* . . . . photo _______________
- ☐ **la pillule** *(pee-lewl)* . . . . pill _______________

(ray-vay)
le réveil

____

J'ai un réveil.

(lar-mwahr)
l'armoire

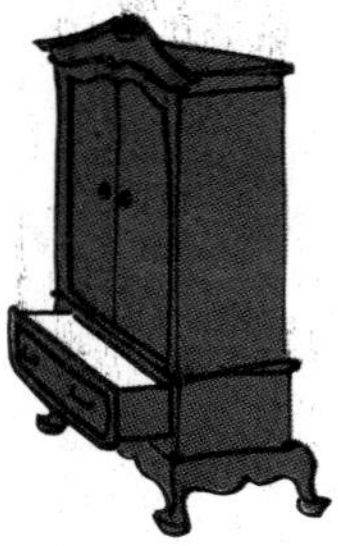

____

(ee-lee-yah)
Il y a (there is) **une armoire dans la chambre.**

Remove the next **cinq** stickers **et** label these **choses dans** your **chambre à coucher.**

La chambre dans un hôtel ou une auberge *(oh-bearzh)* (youth hostel) **de la jeunesse** *(zhuh-ness)* is for sleeping.

dormir = to sleep. This is **un verbe important pour le voyageur** *(vwhy-ah-zhur)* **fatigué** (fatigued). Study **les questions et les réponses suivantes** based on **l'image à gauche.**

1. **Où est le réveil?**

   Le réveil est sur la table.

2. **Où est la couverture?**

   La couverture est sur le lit.

3. **Où est l'armoire?**

   L'armoire est dans la chambre.

4. **Où est l'oreiller?**

   L'oreiller est sur le lit.

5. **Où est le lit?**

   Le lit est dans la chambre.

6. **Le lit est-il** (is it) **grand** (big) **ou petit** *(puh-tee)* (small)**?**

   Le lit n'est pas (not) **grand.**

   Le lit est petit.

- ☐ **le pique-nique** *(peek-neek)* .... picnic ___________
- ☐ **la place** *(plahs)* .... place, seat ___________
- ☐ **le plaisir** *(play-zeer)* .... pleasure ___________
  - **— Avec plaisir.** .... with pleasure ___________
- ☐ **la police** *(poh-lees)* .... police ___________

Maintenant, vous répondez aux questions based on the previous **image.**

Où est le réveil?  **Où est le lit?** 

Le réveil est ______________________ ______________________

Let's move into **la salle de bain et** do the same thing.

(lah-vah-boh) **le lavabo**	*(doosh)* **la douche**	*(doo-bul-vay-say)* **le W.C.**

le lavabo ______	______	______
Il y a (there is) **un lavabo dans la salle de bain.**	**La douche n'est pas dans la chambre d'hôtel.**	**Le W.C. n'est pas dans la chambre d'hôtel. Le W.C. et la douche sont dans le couloir.** *(kool-wahr)* (hallway)

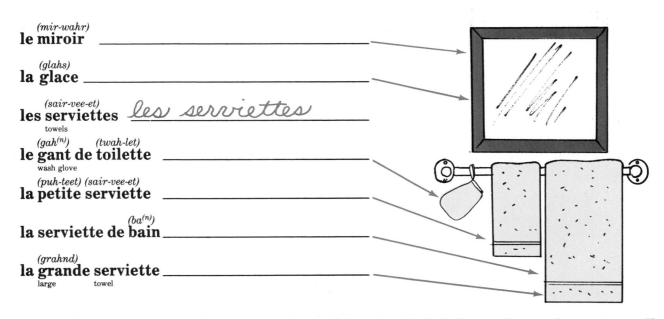

(mir-wahr) **le miroir** ______________________

(glahs) **la glace** ______________________

(sair-vee-et) **les serviettes** (towels) les serviettes ______________________

(gah(n)) *(twah-let)* **le gant de toilette** (wash glove) ______________________

(puh-teet) *(sair-vee-et)* **la petite serviette** ______________________

(ba(n)) **la serviette de bain** ______________________

(grahnd) **la grande** (large) **serviette** (towel) ______________________

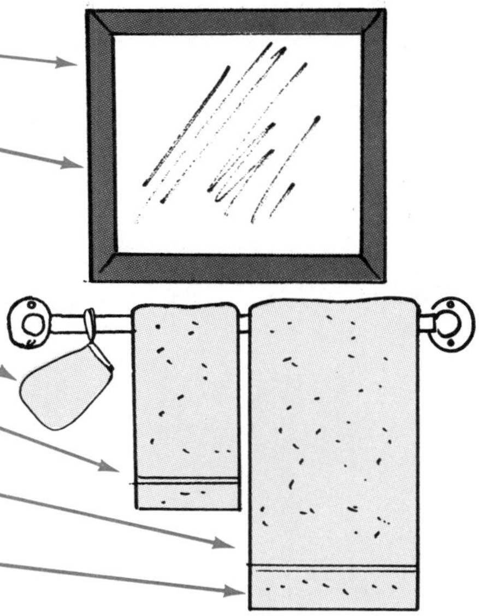

Do not forget to remove **les sept** stickers **suivants et** label these **choses dans** your **salle de bain.**

☐ **la politesse** *(poh-lee-tess)*	politeness	______________
☐ **la politique** *(poh-lee-teek)*	politics	______________
☐ **le port** *(por)*	port	______________
☐ **la Préfecture de Police** *(pray-fek-tewr)* .	Police Headquarters	______________
☐ **premier** *(pruh-mee-ay)*	first	______________

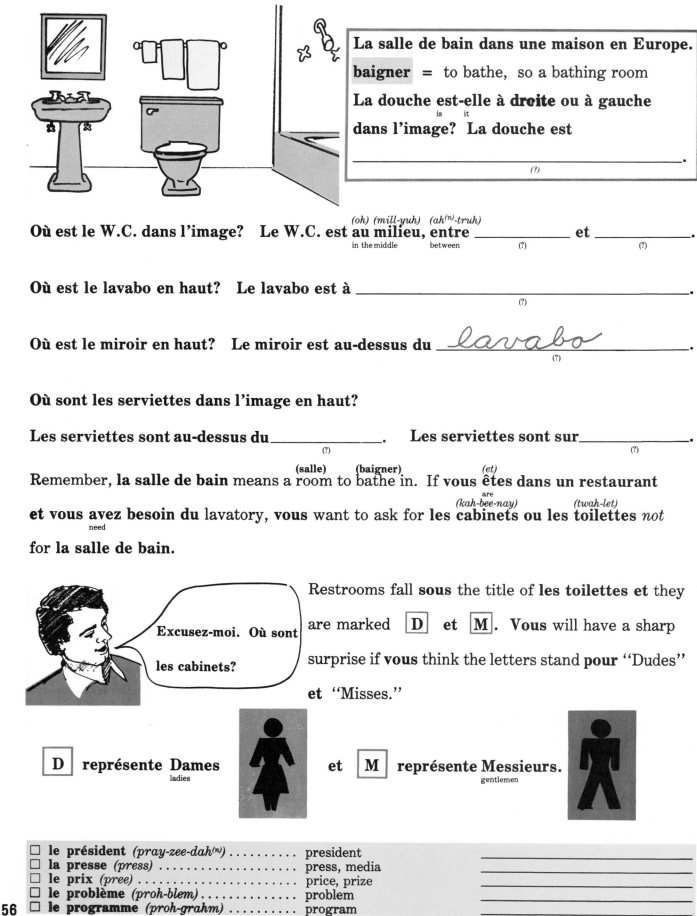

La salle de bain dans une maison en Europe.

baigner = to bathe, so a bathing room

La douche est-elle (is it) **à droite ou à gauche dans l'image? La douche est** ______________________ (?).

Où est le W.C. dans l'image? Le W.C. est au milieu (oh) (mill-yuh), in the middle, **entre** (ah(n)-truh), between, __________ (?) **et** __________ (?).

Où est le lavabo en haut? Le lavabo est à ______________________ (?).

Où est le miroir en haut? Le miroir est au-dessus du ___lavabo___ (?).

Où sont les serviettes dans l'image en haut?

Les serviettes sont au-dessus du __________ (?). **Les serviettes sont sur** __________ (?).

Remember, **la salle de bain** means a room (**salle**) to bathe (**baigner**) in. If **vous êtes** (et), are, **dans un restaurant et vous avez besoin du** (need) lavatory, **vous** want to ask for **les cabinets** (kah-bee-nay) **ou les toilettes** (twah-let) *not* for **la salle de bain.**

Excusez-moi. Où sont les cabinets?

Restrooms fall **sous** the title of **les toilettes et** they are marked **D** **et** **M**. **Vous** will have a sharp surprise if **vous** think the letters stand **pour** "Dudes" **et** "Misses."

D **représente Dames** (ladies)

et **M** **représente Messieurs.** (gentlemen)

- ☐ **le président** *(pray-zee-dah(n))* .... president ______________
- ☐ **la presse** *(press)* .... press, media ______________
- ☐ **le prix** *(pree)* .... price, prize ______________
- ☐ **le problème** *(proh-blem)* .... problem ______________
- ☐ **le programme** *(proh-grahm)* .... program ______________

Next stop — **le** *(bew-row)* **bureau,** specifically **la table ou le bureau** (desk) **dans le bureau!** *(kess)* **Qu'est-ce** (what) *(kee-lee-yah)* **qu'il y a** (is there) **sur le bureau?** Let's identify **les choses** which one normally finds **dans le bureau ou** strewn about **la maison.**

(kray-yoh$^{(n)}$)
le crayon

(stee-low)
le stylo

le stylo

(pah-pee-ay)
le papier

(leh-truh)
la lettre

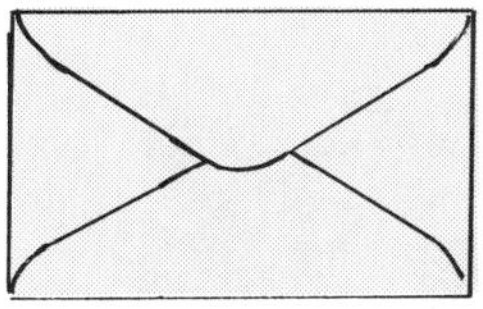

(kart) (pohs-tall)
la carte postale

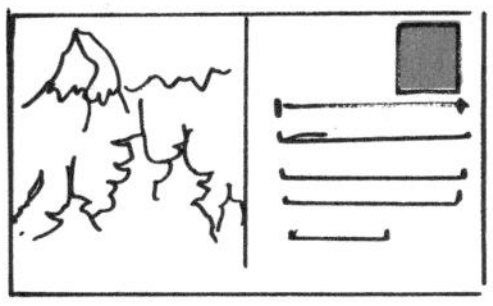

(ta$^{(n)}$-bruh-post)
le timbre-poste

(lee-vruh)
le livre

(ruh-vew) (mahg-ah-zeen)
la revue/le magazine

(zhoor-nahl)
le journal

(lew-net)
les lunettes

(tay-lay-vee-zee-oh$^{(n)}$)
la télévision

(kor-bay) (pah-pee-ay)
la corbeille à papier

- ☐ **le quai** *(kay)* . . . . quay, platform
- ☐ **le quartier** *(kar-tee-ay)* . . . . quarter, district
- ☐ **quatorze** *(kah-torz)* . . . . fourteen
  - **— Louis Quartorze** *(loo-wee)* . . . . Louis the Fourteenth
  - **— le quatorze juillet** *(zhwee-ay)* . . . . July 14th-Independence Day

Maintenant, label these **choses dans le bureau avec** your stickers. Do not forget to say these **mots** out loud whenever **vous les** *(lay)* (them) **écrivez,** *(zay-kree-vay)* (write) **vous** see them **ou vous** apply the stickers. **Maintenant,** identify **les choses en bas** by filling in each blank **avec le mot correct en français.**

1. ____________________
2. ____________________
3. ____________________
4. ____________________
5. le crayon
6. ____________________
7. ____________________
8. ____________________
9. ____________________
10. ____________________

Voilà quatre verbes de plus. *(plews)* (more)

(vwahr) **voir** = to see	*(ah$^{(n)}$-vwhy-ay)* **envoyer** = to send	*(door-meer)* **dormir** = to sleep	*(troo-vay)* **trouver** = to find
____________	____________	dormir	____________

Maintenant, fill in the blanks, **à la** (on) **prochaine** *(pro-shen)* (next) **page, avec la forme** *(form)* (form) **correcte** of these **verbes.** Practice saying the sentences out loud many times.

☐	**le raisin** *(ray-za$^{(n)}$)*	grape	____________
	—le raisin sec *(sek)*	raisin (dried grape)	____________
☐	**la recette** *(ruh-set)*	recipe, receipt	____________
☐	**la récréation** *(ray-kray-ah-see-oh$^{(n)}$)*	recreation	____________
☐	**la région** *(ray-zhee-oh$^{(n)}$)*	region, area	____________

voir

Je vois/ __________ le lit.

Il / Elle voit/ __________ la couverture.

Nous voyons/ __________ l'hôtel.

Vous voyez/ __________ la Tour Eiffel.

Ils / Elles voient/ __________ la douche.

envoyer

J' envoie/ __________ la lettre.

Il / Elle envoie/ __________ la carte postale.

Nous __________ le livre.

Vous __________ quatre cartes postales.

Ils / Elles envoient/ __________ trois lettres.

dormir

Je dors/ __________ dans la chambre.

Il / Elle dort/ __________ dans le lit.

Nous __________ dans l'hôtel.

Vous __________ dans la maison.

Ils / Elles __________ sous la couverture.

trouver

Je __________ le timbre.

Il / Elle trouve/ __________ les journaux.

Nous __________ les lunettes.

Vous __________ le Louvre.

Ils / Elles __________ les fleurs.

Remember that **"oi"** sounds like "wah." Practice **bois** *(bwah)* (drinks), **vois** *(vwah)* (see), **voient** *(vwah)* (see), **envoie** *(ah(n)-vwah)* (sends) and **envoient** *(ah(n)-vwah)* (send). Also, **"ent"** at the end of a verb is silent: **trouve** *(troov)* (finds) and **trouvent** *(troov)* (find).

The expression **n'est-ce pas** *(ness-pah)* is **extrêmement** *(ek-strem-uh-mah(n))* (extremely) useful **en français.** Added onto a sentence, it turns the sentence into a question for which **la réponse** is usually **"oui."** It has only one form and is much simpler than **en anglais.**

C'est un livre, n'est-ce pas? *(ness-pah)*	=	It's a book, isn't it?
Jacqueline est belle, n'est-ce pas?	=	Jacqueline is beautiful, isn't she?
Vous êtes français, n'est-ce pas?	=	You're French, aren't you?

☐ **la Renaissance** *(ruh-nay-sah(n)s)* . . . . rebirth __________
☐ **le rendez-vous** *(rah(n)-day-voo)* . . . . rendezvous, appointment __________
☐ **la république** *(ray-pew-bleak)* . . . . republic __________
— **La Cinquième République** (1958-) the Fifth Republic __________
☐ **la réservation** *(ray-zair-vah-see-oh(n))* . . . reservation __________

Step 15

Le Courrier
(koo-ree-ay) — mail

Vous know **maintenant** how to count, how to ask **questions,** how to use **verbes avec** the "plug-in" formula, how to make statements, **et** how to describe something, be it the location of **un hôtel ou la couleur d'une** *(dewn)* (of a) **maison.** Let's now take the basics that **vous** *(voo)* **avez** *(zah-vay)* learned **et** expand them in special areas that will be most helpful in your travels. What does everyone do on a holiday? Send postcards, **n'est-ce-pas?** *(ness-pah)* Let's learn exactly how **le bureau** *(bew-row)* **de poste** *(post)* (post office) **français (P et T)** works.

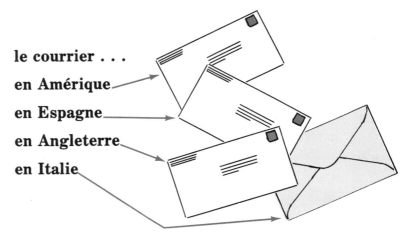

le courrier . . .
en Amérique
en Espagne
en Angleterre
en Italie

Les *(lay)* **P et T** *(pay-ay-tay)* (post office) **(Poste et Télécommunications)** is where you need to go **en France** to buy a stamp, mail a package, send a telegram or use the telephone. **Voilà** some **mots nécessaires** *(nay-say-sair)* (necessary) **pour le bureau de poste.**

la lettre

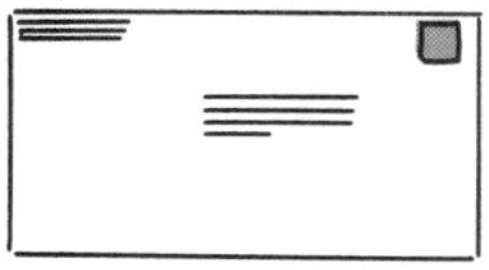

la carte postale

le timbre-poste *(ta(n)-bruh-pohst)*

le télégramme *(tay-lay-grahm)*

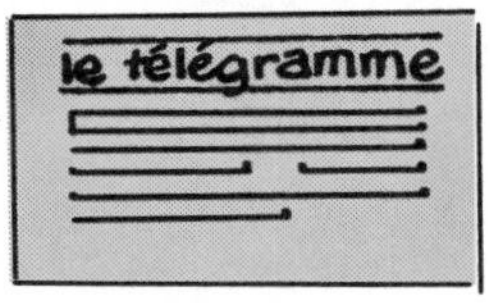

la lettre ____________ ____________ ____________

- ☐ **la résidence** *(ray-zee-dah(n)s)* . . . . residence ____________
- ☐ **la résistance** *(ray-zee-stah(n)s)* . . . . resistance ____________
- ☐ **la révolution** *(ray-voh-lew-see-oh(n))* . . . . . revolution ____________
  - **— 1789 - la Révolution française** . . . . . French Revolution ____________
- ☐ **la route** *(root)* . . . . route, highway ____________

(pah-kay) (koh-lee)
le paquet/le colis

(bwaht) (oh) (let-ruh)
la boîte aux lettres

POSTES

(par) (ah-vee-oh$^{(n)}$)
par avion

PAR AVION
AIR MAIL

par avion

(ge-shay)
le guichet
window/counter

(kah-bean) (tay-lay-phone-eek)
la cabine téléphonique

(tay-lay-phone)
le téléphone

(pay-ay-tay) (bew-row)
les P et T/le bureau de poste

P et T

(oh$^{(n)}$) (too) (ah$^{(n)}$-vwhy-ay)
Les P et T en France ont tout. Vous envoyez les télégrammes, les lettres et les cartes
has / everything / send

(dew)
postales du bureau de poste. Vous achetez les timbres dans le bureau de poste.
from the

(tay-lay-phone-ay) (zhay-nay-rahl-mah$^{(n)}$)
Vous téléphonez du bureau de poste. Le bureau de poste est généralement open from
telephone / generally

(sahm-dee)
8:00 du matin à 7:00 du soir weekdays **et 8:00 à 12:00 le samedi.** If **vous avez besoin**
Saturday / need

(ah-pel)
to call home **en Amérique,** this can be done **au bureau de poste et** is called **un appel**
at the / call

(a$^{(n)}$-tair-ewr-ba$^{(n)}$)
interurbain. Okay. First step — **entrez dans les P et T.**
long distance

(bun) (say)
The following **est une bonne** sample **conversation.** Familiarize yourself **avec ces mots**
these

maintenant.

Excusez-moi.
Où achète-t-on
des timbres?

Au guichet
numéro 7.

GUICHET 7

☐	**le sac** *(sack)*	sack	______
☐	**sacré** *(sah-kray)*	sacred	______
	—Sacré-Coeur à Paris *(sah-kray kur)*	Sacred Heart in Paris	______
☐	**sage** *(sahzh)*	wise, well-behaved	______
☐	**la saison** *(say-zoh$^{(n)}$)*	season	______

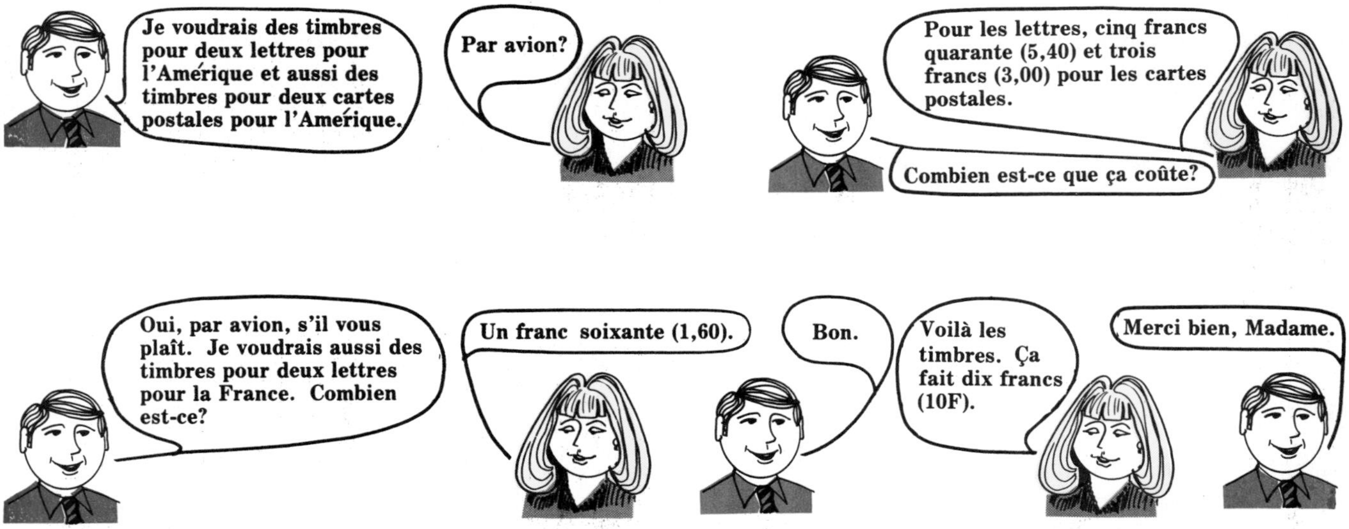

Je voudrais des timbres pour deux lettres pour l'Amérique et aussi des timbres pour deux cartes postales pour l'Amérique.
Par avion?
Combien est-ce que ça coûte?
Pour les lettres, cinq francs quarante (5,40) et trois francs (3,00) pour les cartes postales.
Oui, par avion, s'il vous plaît. Je voudrais aussi des timbres pour deux lettres pour la France. Combien est-ce?
Un franc soixante (1,60).
Bon.
Voilà les timbres. Ça fait dix francs (10F).
Merci bien, Madame.

Next step — **vous** ask **questions** like those **en bas** depending upon what **vous voudriez** *(voo-dree-ay)* [want].

Où est-ce *(ess)* **qu'on** *(koh$^{(n)}$)* [one] **achète** *(nah-shet)* [buy] **des timbres?**

Où est-ce *(ess)* **qu'on** *(koh$^{(n)}$)* **envoie** *(nah$^{(n)}$-vwah)* **un télégramme?**

Où est-ce qu'on achète une carte postale?

Où est-ce qu'on envoie un paquet?

Où est-ce qu'on téléphone?

Où est *(ay)* **la cabine téléphonique?**

Où est-ce qu'on fait un appel *(ah-pel)* [call] **interurbain?** *(a$^{(n)}$-tair-ewr-ba$^{(n)}$)* [long distance]

Combien est-ce que ça coûte?

Où est-ce qu'on fait un appel local? *(low-kahl)*

Où est la boîte aux lettres?

Répétez many times **ces** *(say)* [these] **phrases** *(frahz)* [sentences] **en haut.**

Maintenant, quiz yourself. See if **vous** can translate the following thoughts **en français.**

Les réponses sont en bas de la prochaine *(pro-shen)* [next] **page.**

1. Where is the telephone booth? ______________________________
2. Where does one make a phone call? ______________________________
3. Where does one make a local phone call? ______________________________
4. Where does one make a long-distance phone call? ______________________________
5. Where is the post office? ______________________________

☐ **la salutation** *(sah-lew-tah-see-oh$^{(n)}$)*	greeting	________
☐ **le sandwich** *(sah$^{(n)}$-dweech)*	sandwich	________
☐ **la sauce** *(sohs)*	sauce	________
☐ **le saumon** *(soh-moh$^{(n)}$)*	salmon	________
☐ **la science** *(see-ah$^{(n)}$s)*	science	________

6. Where does one buy stamps? ______________________

7. How much is it? ______________________

8. Where does one send a package? ______________________

9. Where does one send a telegram? ______________________

10. Where is window eight? ______________________

Voilà quatre nouveaux verbes.

(fare) **faire** = to do/make *(moh(n)-tray)* **montrer** = to show *(ay-kreer)* **écrire** = to write *(pay-yay)* **payer** = to pay

______________ ______________ écrire ______________

faire

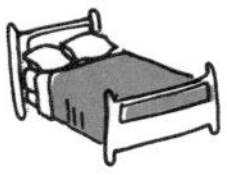

Je fais **un appel.**

Il / Elle fait **le** *(lee)* **lit.** (bed)

Nous faisons **beaucoup.** (a lot)

Vous ne faites **rien.** *(ree-a(n))* (nothing)

Ils / Elles font **tout.** *(too)* (everything)

montrer

Je montre **le livre.**

Il / Elle vous (to you) ______________ **le bureau.**

Nous vous (to you) ______________ **le château.** (castle)

Vous me *(muh)* (to me) ______________ **la lettre.**

Ils / Elles me (to me) ______________ **les P et T.**

écrire

J' écris **une lettre.**

Il / Elle écrit **beaucoup.**

Nous écrivons **un télégramme.**

Vous écrivez **votre signature.** *(voh-truh)(seen-yah-tewr)* (your) (signature)

Ils / Elles n' écrivent **rien.**

payer

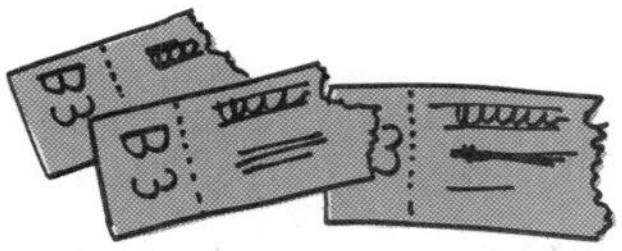

Je paie **l'addition.** *(lah-dee-see-oh(n))* (bill in restaurant)

Il / Elle paie **la taxe.** (tax)

Nous payons **la note.** (bill in hotel)

Vous ______________ **le prix.** *(pree)* (price)

Ils / Elles ne paient **rien.**

RÉPONSES

1. Où est la cabine téléphonique?
2. Où est-ce qu'on téléphone?
3. Où est-ce qu'on fait un appel local?
4. Où est-ce qu'on fait un appel inter(urbain)?
5. Où est le bureau de poste? (les P et T)
6. Où est-ce qu'on achète des timbres?
7. Combien est-ce? Combien est-ce que ça coûte?
8. Où est-ce qu'on envoie un paquet?
9. Où est-ce qu'on envoie un télégramme?
10. Où est le guichet (numéro) huit?

Step 16

Comment *(ko-mah$^{(n)}$)* (how) payer *(pay-yay)* (to pay)

Oui, il y a (there are) **aussi** (also) bills to pay **en France. Vous** have just finished your **repas** *(ruh-pah)* (meal) **délicieux** *(day-lee-see-yuh)* (delicious) **et vous voudriez l'addition** (bill) **et vous voudriez payer. Que faites-vous?** *(fet)* (do you do) **Vous** call for **le serveur** *(sair-vur)* (waiter) **(le garçon)** *(gar-soh$^{(n)}$)* **ou la serveuse** *(sair-vuz)* (waitress).

Bien sûr, Monsieur. Une minute.

Le serveur will normally reel off what **vous** *(voo)* **avez** *(zah-vay)* eaten, while writing rapidly. **Il** will then place **une petite** *(puh-teet)* (little) **feuille** *(fuh-yuh)* (sheet) **de papier sur la table** that looks like **l'addition dans l'image,** while saying something like:

> **"Ça fait** *(fay)* (makes) **vingt-six francs soixante, Monsieur** *(muh-see-uh)***."**

Vous will pay **le serveur** or perhaps **vous** will pay **à** (at) **la caisse** *(kess)* (cashier). Tipping **en France est généralement** much easier than **en Amérique.** If your bill or the menu is marked **"Service** *(sair-vees)* (service) **compris,"** *(koh$^{(n)}$-pree)* (included) then your tip has already been included in your bill. If not, then a 15% tip left **sur la table** is customary. Most French eating establishments are **"Service compris,"** but don't forget to look. You might find some that are **"Service non** (not) **compris."**

Excellent dîner. Merci.
(eel-nee-ah)(pah) (kwah)
Il n'y a pas de quoi.
you're welcome
Au revoir, Monsieur.

- ☐ **second** *(suh-goh$^{(n)}$)* . . . . second ________
- ☐ **le/la secrétaire** *(suh-kray-tair)* . . . . secretary ________
- ☐ **la sécurité** *(say-kew-ree-tay)* . . . . security ________
- ☐ **le sentiment** *(sah$^{(n)}$-tee-mah$^{(n)}$)* . . . . feeling ________
- ☐ **la situation** *(see-tew-ah-see-oh$^{(n)}$)* . . . . situation ________

Remember these key **mots** when dining out **à la française** *(frah(n)-sez)* [in the French manner].

le menu *(muh-new)* or **la carte** *(kart)*	**le pourboire** *(poor-bwahr)* [tip]
l'addition *(lah-dee-see-oh(n))*	**service compris**

La politesse *(poh-lee-tess)* [politeness] **est très importante en France.** You will feel more **français** if you practice and use **ces** *(say)* [these] **expressions** *(zek-spreh-see-oh(n))* [expressions].

excusez-moi or **pardon**

s'il vous plaît

merci beaucoup *(boh-koo)* or **merci bien** *(bee-a(n))*

il n'y a pas de quoi *(eel) (nee-ah) (pah) (duh) (kwah)* [you're welcome/it's nothing]

Voilà une sample **conversation** involving paying **la note** *(note)* [bill] when leaving **un hôtel.**

Jeannette:	**Excusez-moi, Monsieur. Voudriez-vous** *(voo-dree-ay-voo)* [would you] **me préparer** *(muh)(pray-pah-ray)* [for me prepare] **la note?**
L'Hôtelier *(low-tell-ee-ay)* [hotelkeeper]:	**Quelle** *(kel)* [what] **chambre, s'il vous plaît?**
Jeannette:	**Numéro trois cent dix.**
L'Hôtelier:	**Merci. Une minute, s'il vous plaît.**
L'Hôtelier:	**Voilà la note. Ça fait quatre-vingt-dix francs vingt.**
Jeannette:	**Merci beaucoup (et Jeannette** hands him **un billet de cent francs. L'Hôtelier** returns shortly **et dit** *(dee)* [says]**)**
L'Hôtelier:	**Voilà votre** *(voh-truh)* [your] **reçu** *(ruh-sue)* [receipt] **et votre monnaie** [money] **(9F,8). Merci et au revoir** *(oh) (ruh-vwahr)* [goodbye]**.**

Simple, right? If **vous avez** any **problème avec les nombres,** just ask the person to write out **la somme** *(sohm)* [sum] so that **vous** can be sure you understand everything correctly.

"S'il vous plaît, écrivez-moi *(ay-kree-vay-mwah)* [write for me] **la somme** [sum]**. Merci."**

Let's take a break from **l'argent et,** starting **à la prochaine page,** learn some **nouveaux** fun **mots.**

- ☐ **le ski** *(ski)* . . . . skiing ________
- — **le ski-nautique** *(ski-no-teek)* . . . . water skiing ________
- ☐ **la Sorbonne** *(sore-bun)* . . . . part of University of Paris ________
- ☐ **la soupe** *(soup)* . . . . soup ________
- ☐ **le spectacle** *(spek-tah-kluh)* . . . . spectacle, performance ________

Il est en bonne forme.

Il est malade. *(mah-lahd)* — sick

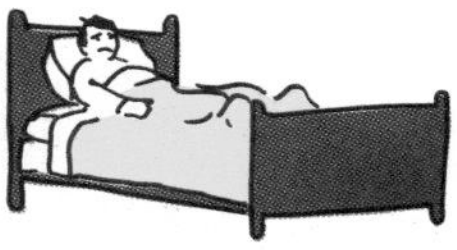

C'est bon. *(boh$^{(n)}$)* — good

Ce n'est pas bon. *(suh) (nay) (pah) (boh$^{(n)}$)* — not

C'est mauvais. *(mow-vay)* — bad

L'eau est chaude. *(showd)* — warm

Elle a 50 degrés. — has

L'eau est froide. *(fwahd)* — cold

Elle a 17 degrés.

Vous parlez fort. *(for)* — loudly

Nous parlons doucement. *(deuce-mah$^{(n)}$)* — softly

La ligne rouge est courte. *(koort)*

La ligne bleue est longue. *(lohng)*

La femme est grande.

L'enfant est petite.

Le livre rouge est gros. *(grow)* — thick

Le livre vert est mince. *(ma$^{(n)}$s)* — thin

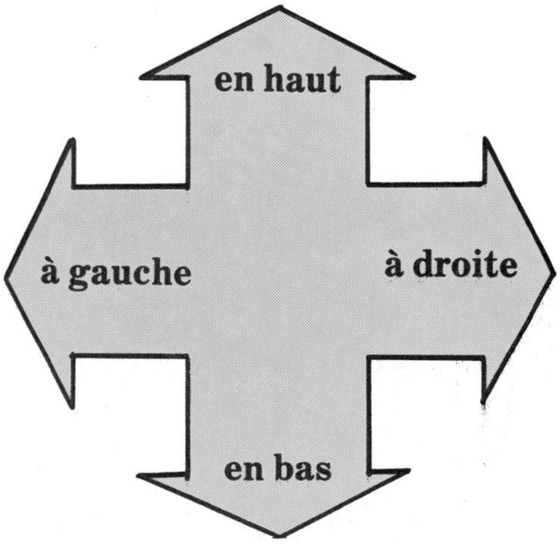

20 kilomètres à l'heure *(ah) (luhr)* — per hour

lent *(lah$^{(n)}$)* — slow

200 kilomètres à l'heure

vite/rapide *(veet) (rah-peed)* — fast

☐ **le sport** *(spor)*	sport	______
☐ **stopper** *(stow-pay)*	to stop	______
☐ **stupide** *(stew-peed)*	stupid	______
☐ **la Suède** *(sue-ed)*	Sweden	______
☐ **la Suisse** *(swees)*	Switzerland	______

(moh$^{(n)}$-tan-yuh) (oht) (meh-truh)
Les montagnes sont hautes. Elles ont 2000 mètres de haut.
mountains high have meters

(bahs)
Les montagnes sont basses. Elles sont seulement 800 mètres de haut.
low

(vee-yuh) (ah$^{(n)}$)
Le grand-père est vieux. Il a soixante-dix ans.
old has years

(zhun)
L'enfant est jeune. Il a seulement dix ans.
young

(share)
La chambre d'hôtel est chère. Elle coûte 94,50 F.
expensive

(lah-zhee) (boh$^{(n)}$)(mar-shay)
La chambre de l'AJ est bon marché. Elle coûte 30,50 F.
youth hostel inexpensive

(reesh) (boh-koo)
J'ai 2.000 F. Je suis riche. C'est beaucoup d'argent.
rich a lot

(poh-vruh) (puh)
Il a seulement 4F. Il est pauvre. C'est peu d'argent.
poor little

Voilà de nouveaux verbes.
some

(sah-vwahr) **savoir** = to know (a fact, an address, etc.)	(poo-vwahr) **pouvoir** = to be able to/can	(duh-vwahr) **devoir** = to have to/must/to owe	(leer) **lire** = to read
____________	____________	devoir	____________

Les verbes "savoir," "pouvoir" et "devoir," along with **le verbe "vouloir,"** can be joined with another **verbe:**

nous savons trouver l'adresse
know how, to find
nous savons parler français

nous pouvons parler
can, speak
nous pouvons comprendre
understand

nous devons payer
must, pay
nous devons manger
eat

☐ **supérieur** *(sue-pay-ree-ur)*	superior, upper	____________
☐ **le surprise** *(sewr-preez)*..............	surprise	____________
☐ **sympathique** *(sa$^{(n)}$-pah-teek)*..............	likeable, nice	____________
— **Qu'il est sympa!** *(kee-lay)*	Oh, he's so nice.	____________
☐ **le système** *(see-stem)*	system	____________

Study their pattern closely as **vous** will use **beaucoup** (a lot) **de ces** (*(say)* these) **verbes.**

savoir

Je sais/ **tout.** (everything)
Il / Elle sait/ **l'adresse.**
Nous savons/ **parler français.**
Vous ______ **commander une bière.**
Ils / Elles ne (do not) savent/ **pas l'adresse.**

pouvoir

Je peux/ **parler français.**
Il / Elle peut/ **comprendre l'anglais.**
Nous pouvons/ **boire.**
Vous pouvez/ **entrer.**
Ils / Elles peuvent/ **parler français aussi.**

devoir

Je dois/ **payer la note.**
Il / Elle doit/ **rester à l'hôtel.**
Nous devons/ **visiter Paris.**
Vous nous (to us) devez/ **5 francs.**
Ils / Elles doivent/ **payer l'addition.**

lire

Je lis/ **le livre.**
Il / Elle lit/ **le journal.**
Nous lisons/ **le menu.**
Vous lisez/ **beaucoup.**
Ils / Elles lisent/ **tout.**

Pouvez-vous translate these thoughts **en bas en français? Les réponses sont en bas.**

1. I can speak French. ______
2. He must pay now. ______
3. We don't know the address. ______
4. You owe us ten francs. Vous nous devez dix francs.
5. She knows everything. ______
6. I am able to speak a little French. ______

RÉPONSES

1. Je peux parler français. **2. Il doit payer maintenant.** **3. Nous ne savons pas l'adresse.** **4. Vous nous devez dix francs.** **5. Elle sait tout.** **6. Je peux parler un peu de français.**

Maintenant, draw **des lignes** *(leen-yuh)* **entre** the opposites **en bas.** Don't forget to say them out loud. Use **ces mots** every day to describe **les choses dans votre** *(voh-truh)* your **maison, dans votre école,** *(ay-kohl)* school at work, etc.

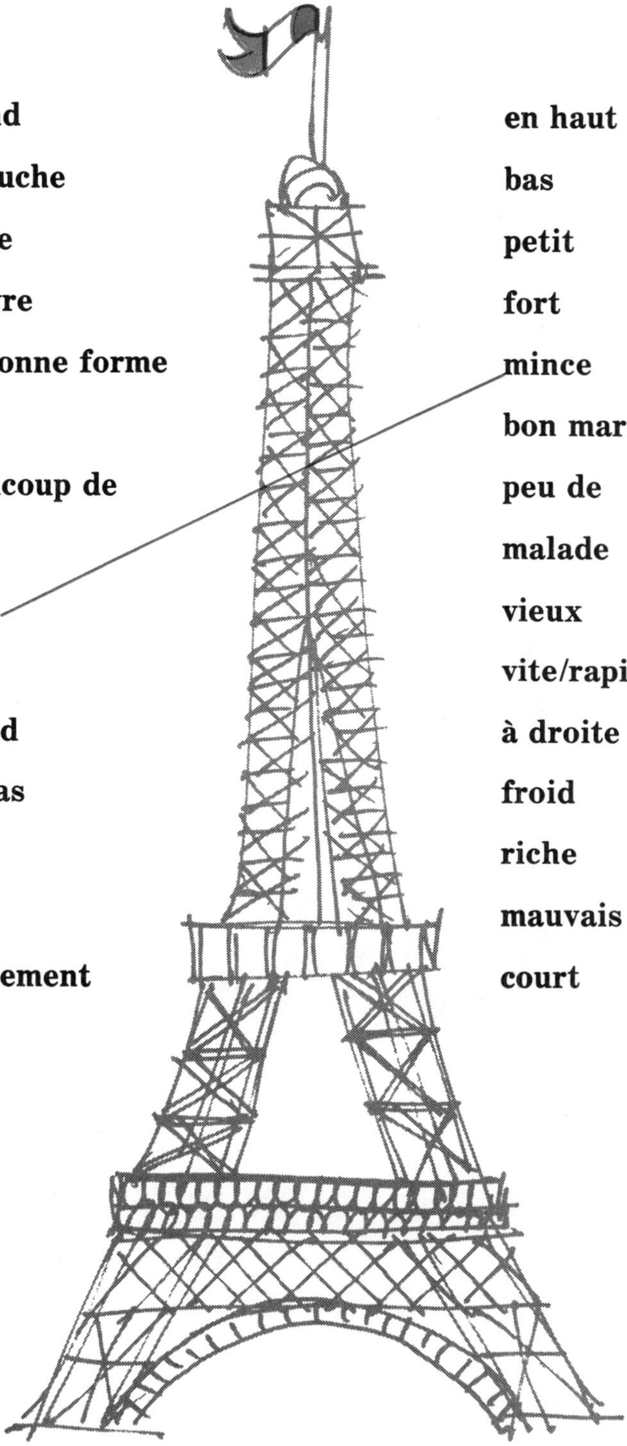

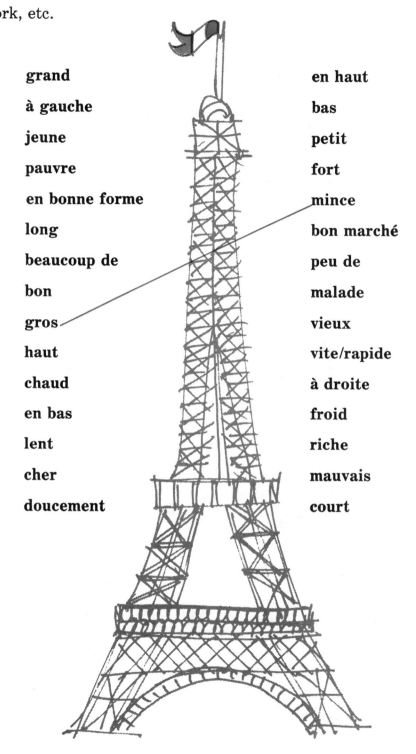

grand	**en haut**
à gauche	**bas**
jeune	**petit**
pauvre	**fort**
en bonne forme	**mince**
long	**bon marché**
beaucoup de	**peu de**
bon	**malade**
gros	**vieux**
haut	**vite/rapide**
chaud	**à droite**
en bas	**froid**
lent	**riche**
cher	**mauvais**
doucement	**court**

☐ **le tabac** *(tah-bah)* .... tobacco ____________
  — le bureau de tabac .... tobacco shop ____________
☐ **la tapisserie** *(tah-pee-suh-ree)* .... tapestry, wall-paper ____________
☐ **le tarif** *(tah-reef)* .... tariff, fare ____________
☐ **le tennis** *(teh-nees)* .... tennis ____________

Step 17

Le Voyageur *(vwhy-ah-zhur)* [traveler] Voyage *(vwhy-ahzh)* [travels]

Hier à Bordeaux! **Aujourd'hui à Tours!** **Demain à Paris!**

Lundi à Dijon! **Mercredi à Marseille!** **Vendredi à Nice!**

Traveling **est** easy, clean **et** efficient **en France. La France n'est pas très grande,** in fact, it is slightly smaller than the state of Texas. **Donc** *(doh$^{(n)}$k)* [therefore], **le voyage est très facile** *(fah-seal)* [easy] within the inviting hexagon **qui** *(key)* [which] **s'appelle** *(sah-pel)* [is called] **la "France." Comment voyager en France?**

Etienne voyage en auto.

Colette voyage en train.

Françoise voyage par avion.

Marie-Anne voyage par bateau.

Xavier et Lucette voyagent en bicyclette à travers [across] **la France.**

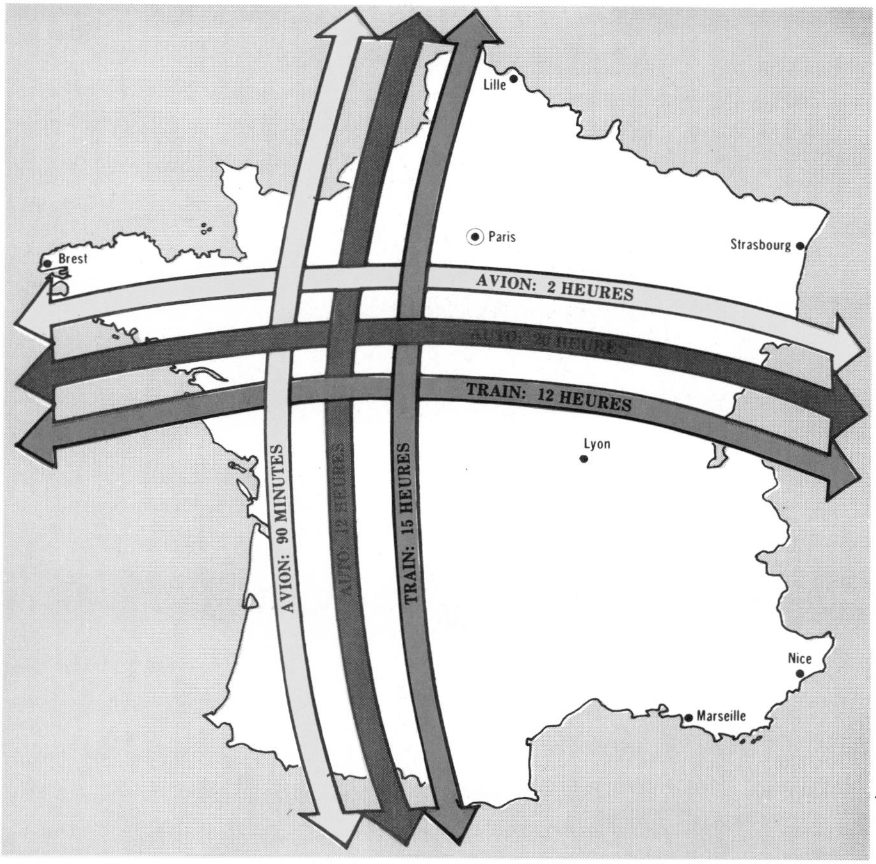

Regardez la carte à gauche. C'est la France, n'est-ce pas *(ness-pah)***? Pour voyager du nord au sud, il faut seulement 90 minutes en avion, 12 heures en auto et 15 heures en train. Pas** *(pah)* [not] **mal** *(mahl)* [bad]**, n'est-ce pas?**

- ☐ **la terrasse** *(tay-rahs)* . . . . terrace, sidewalk cafe
- ☐ **thermal** *(tair-mahl)* . . . . thermal
  - — **les eaux thermales** *(lay-zoh)* . . . . hot springs
- ☐ **le théâtre** *(tay-ah-truh)* . . . . theater
- ☐ **le ticket** *(tee-kay)* . . . . ticket, check

Les Français adorent *(ah-door)* love **voyager,** to travel so it is no **surprise** *(sewr-preez)* to find **beaucoup de mots** built on **le mot "voyage"** *(vwhy-ahzh)* which means "journey" or "trip." Practice saying **les mots suivants** many times. **Vous** will see them **souvent.** *(soo-vah(n))* often

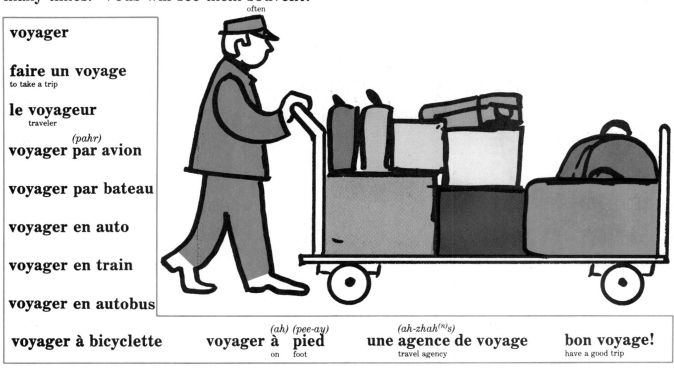

voyager

faire un voyage — to take a trip

le voyageur — traveler

voyager par avion *(pahr)*

voyager par bateau

voyager en auto

voyager en train

voyager en autobus

voyager à bicyclette **voyager à pied** *(ah) (pee-ay)* on foot **une agence de voyage** *(ah-zhah(n)s)* travel agency **bon voyage!** have a good trip

En bas il y a some basic signs which **vous devez** *(duh-vay)* should also learn to recognize quickly. Most of **ces mots** come from **les verbes, entrer** *(ah(n)-tray)* = to enter **et sortir** *(sor-teer)* = to go out.

l'entrée *(lah(n)-tray)* entrance ____________________

l'entrée principale *(pra(n)-see-pahl)* main entrance ____________________

l'entrée latérale *(lah-tay-rahl)* side entrance ____________________

la sortie *(sor-tee)* exit ___la sortie___

la sortie principale main exit ____________________

la sortie de secours *(suh-koor)* emergency exit ____________________

défense d'entrer *(day-fah(n)s) (dah(n)-tray)* do not enter ____________________

entrée interdite *(a(n)-tair-deet)* do not enter ____________________

☐ **le tour** *(tour)*	circumference, tour	____________
— Le Tour de France	bicycle race in France	____________
☐ **la tour** *(tour)*	tower	____________
☐ **tricolore** *(tree-ko-lor)*.............	tricolored	____________
— le drapeau tricolore *(drah-poh)* ..	French flag **(bleu, blanc, rouge)**	____________

(ah-lay) **Aller** (to go) **est un verbe très important pour le** *(vwhy-ah-zhur)* **voyageur** (traveler). If you choose to **aller en automobile,** here are a few key **mots.**

(low-toe-root) **l'autoroute** (freeway) l'autoroute

(koh⁽ⁿ⁾-trah-vah⁽ⁿ⁾-see-oh⁽ⁿ⁾) **une contravention** (ticket) ________________

(root) **la route d'Avignon** (road to Avignon) ________________

(vwah-tewr) (loo-ay) **une voiture à louer** (rental car) ________________

(ah-zhah⁽ⁿ⁾s) (low-kah-see-oh⁽ⁿ⁾) **une agence de location** (car rental agency) ________________

une automobile à louer ________________

Voilà quatre opposites **très importants.**

PARIS-ORLEANS-TOURS-BORDEAUX

km			4087 Exp 1 2	7043 1 2	4055 Exp 1 2	4001 Rap 1 2	4325 Exp 1 2	5 1 R	4031 Rap 1 2	14-003 1 2	313 Rap 1 2	4003 Rap 1 2	4057 Exp 1 2	7045 1 2	4775 Exp 1 2	4059 Exp 1 2	7025 1 2	4005 Rap 1 2	4011 Exp 1 2	4063 Exp 1 2
			⊠	⚒	⚒	⚒ ◆	◆	◆ ✕	◆ ✕	◆	◆ ⊗	◆ ✕			◆	⚒	◆	⊗	◆ ⊗	◆
0	Paris (Austerlitz)	dep.	6 15	..	..	6 45	7 05	7 50	8 03	8 39	9 00	9 09	9 06	..	1000	1015	..	1124	1206	1315
119	Les Aubrais	arr.	|	..	..	|	8 10	|	9 00	|	|	|	1007	..	1102	1112	..	|	1307	1414
121	Orléans	arr.	7 17	..	..	|	8 20	|	9 08	|	|	|	1015	..	1109	1118	..	|	1315	1420
		dep.	7 23	..	7 46	|	8 06	|	8 51	|	|	|	1011	..	1056	1124	1133	|	1302	
119	Les Aubrais	dep.	|	..	7 57	|	8 14	|	9 02	|	|	|	1020	..	1104	|	|	|	1310	..
173	Blois	dep.	7 54	..	8 37	|	8 47	|	|	|	|	|	1105	..	1137	1155	1250	|	1344	..
210	Amboise	dep.	|	..	8 58	|	|	|	|	|	|	|	1128	..	|	|	1320	|	|	..
232	St. Pierre-des-Corps	arr.	8 20	..	9 09	8 28	9 15	9 23	9 52	1034	|	1100	1141	..	1205	1220	1342	1311	1411	..
235	Tours	arr.	8 27	..	9 16	8 37	9 22	9 31	1001	1044	|	1111	1147	..	1213	1227	1348	1321	1422	..
		dep.	..	6 06	..	8 18	..	9 15	9 45	1024	|	1052	..	1216	1158	..		1301	1412	..
232	St. Pierre-des-Corps	dep.	..	|	..	8 30	..	9 24	9 55	1036	|	1103	..	|	1208	..	..	1312	1424	..
300	Châtellerault	dep.	1 2	7 09	..	9 04	..	|	1030	|	|	|	..	1319	1247	..	..	|	1502	..
332	Poitiers	arr.	⚒	7 52	..	9 22	..	1001	1048	1127	|	1149	..	1354	1307	..	..	1359	1522	..
		dep.	5 43		..	9 24	..	1002	1052	1134	|	1153	..	..	1312	..	..	1403	1527	..
445	Angoulême	arr.	7 31	..	..	1015	..	1050	1144	1230	|	1245	..	..	1415	..	1 2	1455	1631	..
		dep.	7 32	..	4833	1017	..	1051	1146	1232	|	1248	..	..	1427	..	1326	1457	1635	4843
528	Coutras 148	dep.	8 34	..	Exp	|	..	|	|	|	|	|	..	..	r	4047	1427	|	1716	Exp
544	Libourne 148	dep.	8 47	..	1 2	1104	..	|	1234	1324	|	1338	..	..	..	Exp	1439	|	1730	1 2
581	Bordeaux (St. Jean)	arr.	9 13	..	†	1126	..	1153	1256	1347	1323	1400	..	..	..	1 2	1501	1605	1752	◆
				5479	♀											◆				
		dep.	..	Exp	1130	1130	..	..	..	1352	1327	1405	..	..	..	1648	..	..	..	1740
690	Morcenx	dep.	5485	1 2	1225	|	..	..	..	|	|	|	..	..	..	1749	..	..	..	|

(lah-ree-vay) **l'arrivée** (arrival) ________________

(day-par) **le départ** (departure) le départ

(lay-trah⁽ⁿ⁾-zhay) **à l'étranger** (foreign) ________________

(la⁽ⁿ⁾-tay-ree-ur) **à l'intérieur** (domestic) ________________

Let's learn the basic **verbes de** *(vwhy-ahzh)* **voyage.** Follow the same pattern you have in previous Steps.

(prah⁽ⁿ⁾-druh)(lah-vee-oh⁽ⁿ⁾) **prendre l'avion** = to take a plane/ to fly

____

(ah-tair-ear) **atterrir** = to land

atterrir

(ray-zair-vay) **réserver** = to reserve/to book

____

(ah-ree-vay) **arriver** = to arrive

____

(par-teer) **partir** = to leave

____

(koh⁽ⁿ⁾-dweer) **conduire** = to drive

____

(moh⁽ⁿ⁾-tay) **monter** = to board/ to climb into

____

(day-bar-kay) **débarquer** = to disembark/ to get out

____

(shah⁽ⁿ⁾-zhay) **changer de train** = to transfer (trains)

____

- ☐ **unique** *(ew-neek)* .... sole, only, single ________________
  - **— enfant unique** *(ah⁽ⁿ⁾-fah⁽ⁿ⁾ tew-neek)* .. only child ________________
- ☐ **universel** *(ew-nee-vair-sell)* .... universal ________________
- ☐ **l'université** *(lew-nee-vair-see-tay)* ...... university ________________
- ☐ **l'urgence** *(lewr-zhah⁽ⁿ⁾s)* .... urgency ________________

Avec ces verbes, vous *(et)* **êtes** ready for any **voyage** anywhere. **Vous** should have no **problèmes avec les verbes,** just remember the basic "plug-in" formula **nous** learned already. Use that knowledge to translate the following thoughts **en français. Les réponses sont en bas.**

1. I fly to Paris. ______________________________
2. I transfer trains in Toulon. ______________________________
3. He lands in Marseille. ______________________________
4. We arrive tomorrow. ______________________________
5. You get off in Tours. ______________________________
6. They travel to Strasbourg. ______________________________
7. Where is the train to Lyon? ______________________________
8. How can one go to Switzerland? With TWA or Air France? ______________________________

____

Voilà de (some) **nouveaux mots pour votre voyage.** As always, write out **les mots et** practice the sample *(frahz)* **phrases** (sentences) out loud.

(kay) **le quai** (platform)

____

Pardon. Où est le quai numéro deux?

(gar) **la gare** (train station)

____

Pardon. Où est la gare?

(lah-ay-row-por) **l'aéroport** (airport)

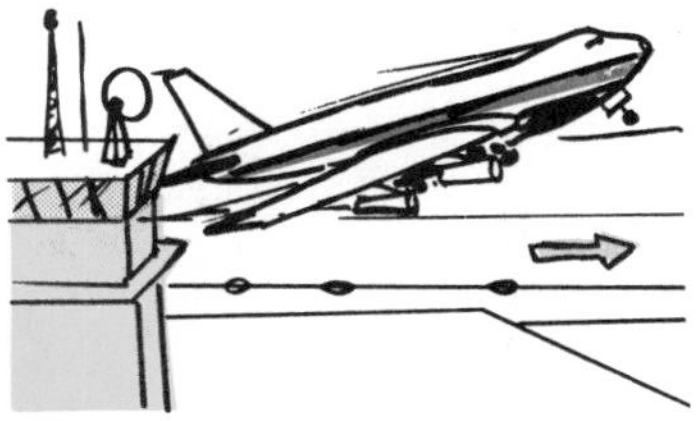

____

Pardon. Où est l'aéroport?

RÉPONSES

1. **Je prends l'avion à Paris.**
2. **Je change de train à Toulon.**
3. **Il atterrit à Marseille.**
4. **Nous arrivons demain.**
5. **Vous débarquez à Tours.**
6. **Ils voyagent à Strasbourg.**
7. **Où est le train pour Lyon?**
8. **Comment peut-on aller en Suisse? Avec TWA ou Air France?**

(bew-row) *(shah$^{(n)}$zh)*
le bureau de change
money-exchange office

(day) *(zohb-zhay)* *(troo-vay)*
le bureau des objets trouvés
lost-and-found office

(low-rare) *(ess-n-say-ef)*
l'horaire (de SNCF)
timetable of French railroad

PARIS—ORLEANS—TOURS

0	Paris (Austerlitz)	dep.	6 15	..	..	6 45	7 05	7 50	8 03	8 39	9 00
119	Les Aubrais	arr.		..	..		8 10		9 00		
121	Orléans	arr.	7 17	..	..		8 20		9 08		
		dep.	7 23	..	7 46		8 06		8 51		
119	Les Aubrais	dep.		..	7 57		8 14		9 02		
173	Blois	dep.	7 54	..	8 37		8 47				
210	Ambroise	dep.		..	8 58						
232	St. Pierre-des-Corps	arr.	8 20	..	9 09	8 28	9 15	9 23	9 52	1034	
235	Tours	arr.	8 27	..	9 16	8 37	9 22	9 31	1001	1044	
		dep.	..	6 06	..	8 18	..	9 15	9 45	1024	

____

Pardon. Où est le bureau de change?

____

Pardon. Où est le bureau des objets trouvés?

____

Pardon. Où est l'horaire?

(oh-kew-pay)
occupé (une place occupée) ____________________
occupied

(lee-bruh)
libre ____________________
free

(koh$^{(n)}$-par-tuh-mah$^{(n)}$)
le compartiment ____________________
compartment

(plahs)
la place la place
seat

(set) *(ay-tell)*
Cette place est-elle occupée? ____________________
this is it

Cette place est-elle libre? ____________________

(suh) *(ay-teel)*
Ce compartiment est-il occupé? ____________________
this is it

Ce compartiment est-il libre? ____________________

Practice writing out **les questions suivantes.** It will help you **plus tard.** *(plew) (tar)* later

Excusez-moi. Où sont les toilettes? ____________________

(vah-goh$^{(n)}$) *(res-toe-rah$^{(n)}$)*
Excusez-moi. Où est le wagon-restaurant? ____________________
dining car

(sahl) *(dah-tah$^{(n)}$t)*
Où est la salle d'attente? Où est la salle d'attente?
room waiting

(ge-shay)
Où est le guichet numéro huit? ____________________

(a$^{(n)}$-tair-dee) *(few-may)*
Est-ce interdit de fumer? ____________________
is it prohibited to smoke

☐	**les vacances** *(vah-kah$^{(n)}$s)*	vacation, holidays	____________
	— les grandes vacances	summer vacation	____________
☐	**la valse** *(valse)*	waltz	____________
☐	**la vanille** *(vah-nee-yuh)*	vanilla	____________
	— la glace à la vanille *(glahs)*	vanilla ice cream	____________

Increase your **mots de voyage** by writing out **les mots en bas et** practicing the sample *(frahz)* **phrases** out loud. (sentences)

(ah) **à** (to) ____________________
Le train est-il à Paris?

(tah(n)) **temps** (time) ____________________
J'ai très peu de temps.

(vwah) **la voie** (track) ____________________
Le train part de la voie numéro sept.

le bureau de *(rah(n)-sen-yuh-mah(n))* **renseignements** (information bureau) ____________________
____
Où est le bureau de renseignements?

(koh(n)-seen-yuh) **la consigne** (left-luggage office) ____________________

(por-tur) **le porteur** (porter) ____________________

(bee-ay) **le billet** (airplane/train ticket) __le billet__

Practice **ces mots** every day. **Vous** will be surprised how *(soo-vah(n))* **souvent vous** (often) will use them.

Pouvez-vous (can) **lire la leçon suivante?**

> **Vous** *(et)* **êtes maintenant** *(ah-see)* **assis** (seated) **dans l'avion et vous allez en France. Vous avez** exchanged **de l'argent** (you have, haven't you?), **vous avez les billets et le passeport et vous avez les** *(vah-leez)* **valises** (suitcases) all packed. **Vous êtes maintenant touriste. Vous** *(ah-tair-ee-say)* **atterrissez demain à 14:15 en France. Bon voyage! Amusez-vous** *(bee-ya(n))* **bien** (well).

Maintenant, vous have arrived **et vous** head for **la gare** in order to get to **votre** *(day-stee-nah-see-oh(n))(fee-nahl)* **destination finale. Les trains français** come in many shapes, sizes **et** speeds. **Il y a** *(rah-peed)* **le rapide (très rapide),** *(lek-spress)* **l'express (assez** (fairly) **rapide),** *(lome-nee-boos)* **l'omnibus (lent) et** *(low-toe-rye)* **l'autorail (aussi lent).** Some **trains** *(oh(n))* **ont** (have) **un** *(vah-goh(n))* **wagon-restaurant** (dining car) **et** some **trains ont un** *(vah-goh(n)-lee)* **wagon-lit** (sleeping car) **ou des** *(koo-shet)* **couchettes** (berths). All this will be indicated **sur l'horaire,** but remember **vous savez comment** to ask things like this. Practice your possible *(koh(n)-bee-nay-zoh(n))* **combinaisons de questions** (combinations) by writing out the following samples.

Y a-t-il (is there) **un wagon-restaurant dans le train?** ____________________

Y a-t-il des couchettes dans le train? __Y a-t-il__

Y a-t-il un wagon-lit dans le train? ____________________

☐ **la variété** *(vah-ree-ay-tay)*	variety	________
☐ **la veine** *(ven)*	vein (in the body)	________
— **avoir de la veine**	to be lucky	________
☐ **la version** *(vair-see-oh(n))*	version, film translation	________
— **la version originale (VO)** *(oh-ree-zhee-nahl)*	original version (of a film)	________

(pree) (bee-ay) (tah-reef) (for-mew-lay)
What about inquiring about **le prix des billets ou le tarif?** **Vous pouvez formuler des questions.**
price tickets fare formulate

(kohm-bee-yen) (by-own)
Combien est le billet (le tarif) pour Bayonne? ______________________

(ah-lay) (ruh-tour)
aller (one-way) aller______________ **aller et retour** (round-trip) ______________

(bore-doe)
Combien est le billet pour Bordeaux? ______________________

(leel)
Combien est le billet pour Lille? ______________________

Aller ou aller et retour? ______________________

(day-par) (ah-ree-vay)
What about times of **départs et arrivées?** **Vous pouvez formuler ces questions aussi.**
departures arrivals

(gruh-noh-bluh)
A quelle heure part le train pour Grenoble? A quelle______________________
leaves

A quelle heure part l'avion pour Rome? ______________________

(mah-dreed)
A quelle heure arrive le train de Madrid? ______________________
from

A quelle heure arrive l'avion de New York? ______________________

(voo-dree-ay-voo) (zah-lay)
Vous have arrived **en France. Vous êtes maintenant à la gare. Où voudriez-vous aller?**
at the would you like

(bee-ay)
Well, tell that to the person at the **guichet** selling **les billets.**

(bruh-tan-yuh)
Je voudrais aller en Bretagne. ______________________

(eks-ah(n)-pro-vah(n)s)
Je voudrais aller à Aix-en-Provence. ______________________

(vair-sigh)
Nous voudrions aller à Versailles. Nous voudrions aller à Versailles.

A quelle heure part le train pour Nice? ______________________

Combien coûte le billet pour Versailles? ______________________

Je voudrais un billet pour Versailles. ______________________

(pruh-mee-air) (klahs) (duh-zee-em)
première classe (first class) ______________ **deuxième classe** (second class) ______________

Aller ou aller et retour? ______________________

(dwah-zh)
Dois-je changer de train? (must I) ______________ **Merci.** ______________

Avec this practice, **vous êtes** off **et** running. **Ces mots de voyage** will make your holiday twice as enjoyable **et** at least three times as easy. Review **ces nouveaux mots** by doing the crossword puzzle **à la page** 77. Practice drilling yourself on this Step by selecting other locations **et** asking your own **questions** about **les trains, les autobus ou les avions** that go there. Select **de nouveaux mots de votre dictionnaire et** practice asking questions that **commencent** *(ko-mah(n)s)* begin **par** *(par)* by **OÙ** **QUAND** **COMBIEN** **COMBIEN DE FOIS** *(fwah)* how often/how many times **ou** making statements like

Je voudrais aller à Paris.

Je voudrais acheter un billet.

MOTS CROISÉS

ACROSS
1. train station
2. timetable
3. track
4. yes
5. with
6. we/us
7. to smoke
8. information bureau
9. no
10. money
11. platform
12. passport
13. airport
14. free
15. to climb into/board
16. entrance

DOWN
1. to arrive
2. to change trains
3. traveler
4. good trip
5. dining car
6. to disembark
7. exit
8. to go
9. she
10. to leave
11. time
12. nothing

RÉPONSES AUX MOTS CROISÉS

ACROSS
1. gare
2. horaire
3. voie
4. oui
5. avec
6. nous
7. fumer
8. bureau de renseignements
9. non
10. argent
11. quai
12. passeport
13. aéroport
14. libre
15. monter
16. entrée

DOWN
1. arriver
2. changer de train
3. voyageur
4. bon voyage
5. wagon-restaurant
6. débarquer
7. sortie
8. aller
9. elle
10. partir
11. temps
12. rien

Step 18

Le Menu (muh-new) [menu] ou la Carte (kart)

Vous êtes maintenant en France et vous avez (have) une chambre. Et maintenant? Vous avez faim (fa$^{(n)}$) [hunger]**. Vous voudriez manger. Mais** (may) [but]**, où y a-t-il** (ee-ah-teel) [is there] **un bon restaurant?** First of all, **il y a** (eel-ee-ah) [there are] different types of places to eat. Let's learn them.

(res-toe-rah$^{(n)}$) **le restaurant**	=	exactly what it says, with a variety of meals and prices
(brah-suh-ree) **la brasserie**	=	originally a beer-saloon, but now also a restaurant
(low-bairzh) **l'auberge**	=	originally a country inn, but it can be an inviting city restaurant
(bee-stroh) **le bistro**	=	slang for **le bar** or a small, intimate restaurant with lots of atmosphere
le bar	=	like a pub which serves morning pastries but concentrates on liquid refreshments
(kah-fay) **le café**	=	like **le bar,** here you will find mainly drinks served (This is where you want to sip your coffee at the sidewalk table.)
(roo-tee-ay) **le restaurant routier**	=	truck-stop
le snack bar	=	offers a quick meal of sandwiches, quiche, etc., the eating is often done standing up

Try them all. Experiment. **Vous trouvez maintenant un bon restaurant. Vous entrez dans le restaurant et trouvez une place.** Sharing **tables avec** others **est** a common **et très** pleasant **coutume** (koo-tewm) [custom] **en Europe.** If **vous voyez** (vwhy-ay) [see] **une chaise** vacant, just be sure to ask

Excusez-moi. Cette (set) **place est-elle** (ay-tell) [is it] **libre** (lee-bruh)**?**

If **vous avez besoin d'un menu,** catch the attention of **le serveur et** say

Monsieur! Le menu (ou la carte), s'il vous plaît.

- ☐ **la vierge** *(vee-airzh)* . . . . virgin ______
  - **— la Sainte Vierge** *(sa$^{(n)}$t)* . . . . Virgin Mary ______
- ☐ **la vigne** *(veen-yuh)* . . . . grape vine ______
- ☐ **le vigneron** *(veen-yur-oh$^{(n)}$)* . . . . wine-grower ______
- ☐ **le vignoble** *(veen-yuh-no-bluh)* . . . . vineyard ______

En France, il y a trois main **repas** (ruh-pah) meals to enjoy every day, plus **un café et** perhaps **une pâtisserie** (pah-tee-suh-ree) pastry **pour le voyageur fatigué** late in **l'après-midi.**

le petit déjeuner (puh-tee)(day-zhuh-nay)	=	breakfast . . . this is a "continental breakfast," with **café ou thé et** toast **ou croissant.** Be sure to check serving times before retiring.
le déjeuner (day-zhuh-nay)	=	lunch . . . . . . generally served from 12:00 to 14:00. You will be able to find any type of meal, **grand ou petit,** served at this time.
le dîner (dee-nay)	=	dinner . . . . . generally served from 19:30 to 22:00, **les Français** eat much later than Americans. This meal is meant to be relished, surrounded by good friends and a pleasant atmosphere.

If **vous** look around you **dans un restaurant français, vous** will see that some **coutumes** (koo-teuwm) customs **françaises sont différentes** (dee-fay-rah(n)t) from ours. **Le pain** (pa(n)) bread may be set directly on the tablecloth, elbows are often rested **sur la table** and please do not forget to mop up your **sauce avec votre pain! Vous** will hear **"Bon Appétit"** (bun) (ah-pay-tee) before **votre repas et** an inquiring **"C'était bon?"** (say-tay) after **vous** have finished. **Le serveur** is asking if **vous** enjoyed **votre repas et** if it tasted good. A smile **et a "Oui, merci"** will tell him that you enjoyed it.

Maintenant, it may be **petit déjeuner** time **à Denver, mais** (may) but **vous êtes en France et il est 19:00.** Most **restaurants français** post **le menu** outside. Always read it before entering so **vous savez** what type of **repas et prix** (pree) prices **vous** will encounter inside. Most **restaurants** offer **un plat du jour** (plah) (dew) special meal of the day **ou un menu à prix fixe** fixed. This is a complete **repas** at a fair **prix.** In addition, **il y a** all the following main categories **sur le menu.** (muh-new)

- ☐ **le village** *(vee-lahzh)* . . . . village ________________
- ☐ **le vin** *(va(n))* . . . . wine ________________
- ☐ **la visite** *(vee-zeet)* . . . . visit ________________
- ☐ **la vitamine** *(vee-tah-mean)* . . . . vitamin ________________
- ☐ **le vocabulaire** *(voh-kah-bew-lair)* . . . . . . vocabulary ________________

(or-duh-vruh)
hors-d'oeuvres .... appetizers

(po-tahzh) *(soup)*
potages/soupes .... soups

(uh)
oeufs .... eggs and egg dishes

(pwah-soh$^{(n)}$)
poissons .... fish and seafood dishes

(ah$^{(n)}$-tray) *(vee-ah$^{(n)}$nd)*
entrées et viandes .... main dishes and meat dishes

(lay-gewm)
légumes .... vegetables

(sah-lahd)
salades .... salads

(day-sair)
desserts .... desserts

(fwee) *(froh-mahzh)*
—fruit ou fromage .... fruit or cheese

(pah-tee-suh-ree)
—pâtisserie .... pastry

(bwah-soh$^{(n)}$)
boissons .... beverages

Most **restaurants** also offer **les** *(spay-see-ah-lee-tay)* **specialtiés de la maison ou** special meals prepared *(pahr)* **par** (by) *(shef)* **le chef.** And if **vous** are sampling the wine, don't forget to ask about the **vin de la maison** (house wine). **Maintenant** for a preview of delights to come . . . At the back of this **livre vous** *(troo-vay)* **trouvez** a sample **menu français. Lisez le menu aujourd'hui et apprenez les nouveaux mots! Quand vous** are ready to leave for **Europe,** cut out **le menu,** fold it **et** carry it in your pocket, wallet **ou** purse. **Vous** *(poo-vay)* **pouvez** (can) *(zah-lay)* **aller dans** any **restaurant et** feel prepared. (May I suggest studying **le menu** after, **et** not before, **vous avez** eaten!)

Most "w" words are foreign additions to **le français.**

- ☐ **le wagon** *(vah-goh$^{(n)}$)* .... railroad car ______
- ☐ **le week-end** *(week-end)* .... weekend ______
- ☐ **le western** *(wes-tairn)* .... western (film) ______
- ☐ **le whisky** *(we-skee)* .... whisky ______

In addition, learning the following should help you to identify what kind of meat **ou** poultry **vous commandez et comment** it will be prepared.

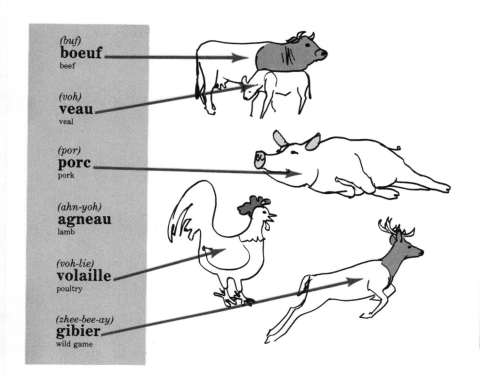

(buf)
boeuf
beef

(voh)
veau
veal

(por)
porc
pork

(ahn-yoh)
agneau
lamb

(voh-lie)
volaille
poultry

(zhee-bee-ay)
gibier
wild game

(kwee)
cuit = cooked

(roh-tee)
rôti = roasted

(free)
frit = fried

(kwee) (toh) (foor)
cuit au four = baked

(gree-ay)
grillé = grilled

(far-see)
farci = stuffed

Vous will also get **légumes** *(lay-gewm)* (vegetables) **avec votre repas et** perhaps **une salade verte** *(vairt)* (green), after **l'entrée.** One day at an open-air **marché** *(mar-shay)* (market) will teach you **les noms** for all the different kinds of **légumes et fruits** *(fwee)*, plus it will be a delightful experience for you. **Vous pouvez** (can) always consult your menu guide at the back of **ce livre** if **vous** *(voo)* **oubliez** *(zoo-blee-ay)* (forget) **le nom correct.** **Maintenant vous avez** decided what **vous voudriez** *(voo-dree-ay)* **manger et le serveur arrive.**

Et comme boisson?
Je voudrais la soupe du jour et une côtelette de porc.
Un verre de vin blanc, s'il vous plaît.

☐ **le zèbre** *(zeh-bruh)*	zebra	______
— **zébré** *(zay-bray)*	striped	______
☐ **le zèle** *(zel)*	zeal, ardor	______
— **zélé** *(zay-lay)*	zealous	______
☐ **le zénith** *(zay-neat)*	zenith, peak	______

(noo-blee-ay) (pah)
N'oubliez pas (don't forget) to treat yourself to **un dessert français.** You would not want to miss out on trying **les desserts suivants.**

(krem) (kah-rah-mel) **une crème caramel** custard with burnt sugar sauce	*(tart) (oh) (pohm)* **une tarte aux pommes** apple pie
(moose) (oh) (show-ko-lah) **une mousse au chocolat** whipped chocolate pudding	*(day) (zah-nah-nah) (oh) (rome)* **des ananas au rhum** pineapple in rum

After completing **votre repas,** call **le serveur et** pay just as **vous avez** already learned in Step 16:

Monsieur, je voudrais l'addition, s'il vous plaît.

En bas il y a une sample **carte** to help you prepare for your holiday.

RESTAURANT
RELAIS DE POSTE

LA CARTE

HORS-D'OEUVRE

Oeufs durs mayonnaise (hard-boiled eggs with mayonnaise)	6,50 F
Salade de tomates (sliced tomatoes)	6,50
Salade niçoise (mixed salad with tuna, green beans and potatoes)	8,00
Filets d'anchois (anchovies)	8,00
Artichaut vinaigrette (artichoke with oil and vinegar sauce)	10,50

POTAGES

Soupe à l'oignon (French onion soup)	8,00
Potage aux asperges (creamed asparagus)	9,50
Bouillabaisse (fish soup)	12,00
Bisque de homard (lobster bisque)	12,00

POISSONS ET FRUITS DE MER

Huîtres (oysters)	32,00
Coquille St. Jacques (scallops)	25,00
Langoustines mayonnaise (boiled lobster with mayonnaise)	35,00
Moules (mussels)	30,00
Sole meunière (fried sole in butter)	28,50

ENTRÉES ET VIANDES

Escalope de veau à la crème (veal cutlets in cream sauce)	50,00
Tournedos bearnaise (beef tenderloin in bearnaise sauce)	50,00
Côtes d'agneau grillé (grilled lamb chops)	38,00
Daube de boeuf (marinated beef pot roast)	40,00
Canard au poivre vert (duck with green peppers)	45,00
Poulet à l'estragon (tarragon chicken)	40,00
Tripes (stomach lining of calf or beef)	35,00

LÉGUMES

Gratin dauphinois (scalloped potatoes)	8,00
Légumes de saison (seasonal vegetables)	9,00
Champignons sautés provençale (sauted mushrooms)	10,50
Salade verte (tossed green salad)	8,00

FROMAGE

Plateau de fromage, par personne (cheese selection)	15,00

DESSERTS

Pâtisserie (pastry from tray)	8,50
Glace à la fraise (strawberry ice cream)	6,50
Corbeille de fruits (choice of fruit)	6,00
Crèpes Suzette (crèpes with liqueur)	15,00
Pêche Melba (peach and vanilla ice cream)	8,50

BOISSONS

Vin (verre)	6,00
Vin (carafe)	15,00
Bière	6,00
Eau minérale (mineral water)	2,50
Limonade	3,00
Jus de fruit (fruit juice)	4,00
Lait	3,00
Café	2,50
Thé	2,50

Service 15% compris

☐ **le zéphyr** *(zay-feer)*	balmy breeze	______
☐ **zéro** *(zay-row)*	zero	______
☐ **le zodiaque** *(zoh-dee-ak)*	zodiac	______
— Je suis de signe "poisson."	I am a "pisces."	______
☐ **la zoologie** *(zoh-oh-loh-zhee)*	zoology	______

Le petit déjeuner est un peu (little) **différent** *(dee-fay-rah^(n))* because it is fairly standardized **et vous** will frequently take it at **votre hôtel** as **il est généralment** included in **le prix de votre chambre. En bas il y a** a sample of what **vous pouvez** expect to greet you **le matin.**

Petit déjeuner - Simple *(sa^(n)-pluh)* 6F

café au lait
coffee and steamed milk
pain

Petit déjeuner - Complet *(koh^(n)-play)* . . . 12F

café au lait

croissants

beurre et confiture
jam

Petit déjeuner à l'anglaise
in the English manner

(these additions usually only available in large hotels catering to foreigners)

jus d'orange

jus de pamplemousse
grapefruit

jambon
ham

saucisse
sausage

oeuf à la coque
egg soft-boiled

oeuf mollet
medium-boiled.

oeufs brouillés
scrambled

omelette nature

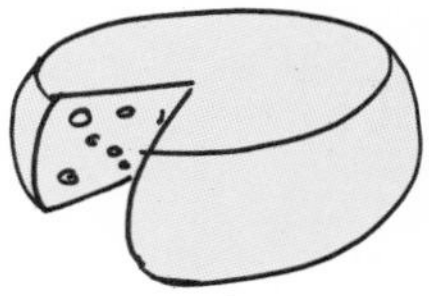

Des phrases pratiques

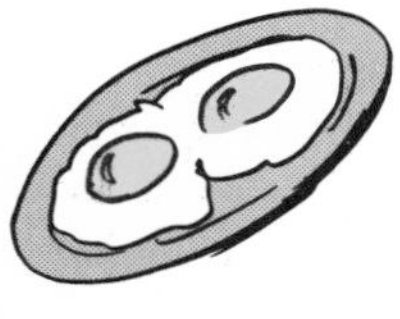

Combien coûte le petit déjeuner?

Je voudrais deux complets, s'il vous plaît.

Je voudrais des croissants et du thé, s'il vous plaît.

Veuillez *(vuh-yay)* (please) **faire** *(fare)* (have) **monter** (brought up) **le petit déjeuner à la chambre dix, s'il vous plaît.**

☐ **la zone** *(zohn)*	zone	______________
— **une zone de silence** *(see-lah^(n)s)*	quiet zone	______________
☐ **le zoo** *(zoh)*	zoo	______________
— **un jardin zoologique**	zoological garden	______________
☐ **Zut!** *(zewt)*	Darn! Rats!	______________

Step 19

Le Téléphone
(tay-lay-phone) telephone

Qu'est-ce (kess) (what) **qui** (key) **est différent** about **le téléphone en France?** Well, **vous** never notice such things until **vous** want to use them. Be warned **maintenant** that **téléphones en France** are much less numerous than **en Amérique.** Nevertheless, **le téléphone** allows you to reserve **les chambres d'hôtel dans** another **ville** (veel) (city), call friends, **demander des renseignements sur les billets de théâtre, de concert ou de ballet,** make emergency calls, check on the hours of a **musée** (mew-zay) (museum), rent **une automobile et** all those other **choses** which **nous faisons** on a daily basis. It also gives you a certain amount of **liberté** (lee-bear-tay) **quand vous pouvez** make your own **appels** (ah-pel) (calls) **de téléphone.**

Having **un téléphone dans votre maison n'est** (is) **pas** (not) as common **en France** as **en Amérique.** That means that **vous devez** (must) **savoir où trouver** (to find) **les téléphones:** in the **bureaux de poste** (post offices), on the street, in the **cafés** and in the lobby of **votre hôtel.** Often **vous devez acheter** a token, called **un jeton** (zhuh-toh(n)), before you use a public **téléphone.**

Voilà un téléphone public français.

So far, so good. **Maintenant,** let's read the instructions for using **le téléphone.** This **est** one of those moments when you realize,

Je ne (nuh) **suis** (swee) (am) **pas** (pah) (not) **en Amérique** (zah(n)).

So let's learn how to operate **le téléphone.**

If **vous** use **le téléphone dans un bar ou un café,** be sure to ask, **"Est-ce** *(ess)* **qu'un** *(kuh$^{(n)}$)* **jeton** *(zhuh-toh$^{(n)}$)* **est nécessaire?"** *(nay-say-sair)* The **bar** employee will sell you **un jeton** to use if it is needed **et,** if not, then **vous pouvez** use regular **pièces de monnaie.**

Consultez le tableau des taxes ci-contre et préparez votre monnaie en fonction du
indicator of prices attached prepare depending upon

temps pendant lequel vous désirez parler, car l'appareil ne rend pas la monnaie.
time during which desire for does not return

Décrochez le combiné et composez le numéro
lift receiver dial

Vous ne pourrez introduire les pièces qu'après la réponse de votre correspondant.
insert coins only after party

Lorsque le demandé a répondu, la tonalité d'appel se transforme en une tonalité
when called party has answered dial tone changes to tone

de paiement (bip-bip-bip . . .)
payment

Introduisez immediatement les pièces.
insert

La tonalité de paiement ne s'arrête et vous ne pouvez parler que lorsque
stops only when

l'appareil a encaissé une somme suffisante.
has registered sum

Pour prolonger la conversation introduisez d'autres pièces,
to lengthen additional

—à n'importe quel moment durant la conversation
at any time during

—très rapidement, dès que vous reentendez la tonalité de paiement (bip-bip-bip)
quickly as soon as hear again

Anglais		Français
telephone	=	**le téléphone**
telephone booth	=	**la cabine téléphonique**
telephone book	=	**l'annuaire** *(lah-new-air)*
telephone conversation	=	**la conversation téléphonique**

Anglais		Français
to telephone	=	**téléphoner**
	=	**faire un appel**
operator	=	**le téléphoniste**
	=	**le standardiste**
token	=	**le jeton**

So **maintenant vous savez comment faire un appel en France. Vous** will find that **la majorité** *(ma-zhoh-ree-tay)* **des** *(day)* **numéros** *(new-may-row)* **en France sont six** digits, such as **47-06-14.** However, **à Paris, il y a sept** digits, such as **326-69-12. Il y a** (there are) **aussi** area codes, or **indicatifs régionaux,** *(a(n)-dee-ka-teef) (ray-zhee-oh-noh)* and these are listed in **l'annuaire** *(lah-new-air)* (telephone book). **Les téléphones dans les maisons** also have an added feature different from ours in that they come equipped with an extra listening device as extension phones are rare.

When answering **le téléphone, vous** pick up **le récepteur** *(ray-sep-tur)* (receiver) **et** say,

"Allô? C'est ______________ (votre nom) à l'appareil." *(ah)(lah-pah-ray)* (on the phone)

When saying good-bye, **vous dites, "A demain"** *(ah)(duh-ma(n))* (till tomorrow) **ou "Au revoir."** *(oh) (ruh-vwahr)* (good-bye) **Voilà** some sample **conversations au** (on the) **téléphone.** Write them in the blanks **en bas.**

Je voudrais téléphoner au Louvre. *(loo-vruh)* ______________________________

Je voudrais téléphoner à Chicago. Je voudrais téléphoner à Chicago.

Je voudrais téléphoner à Madame Le Gaul à Marseille. ______________________________

Je voudrais téléphoner à Monsieur Le Gaul à Nice. ______________________________

Je voudrais téléphoner à Air France à l'aéroport. ______________________________

Je voudrais faire *(fare)* (make) **un appel en P.C.V.** *(pay-say-vay)* (collect call) ______________________________

Où est la cabine téléphonique? ______________________________

Où est l'annuaire? ______________________________

Mon numéro est 68-70-10. ______________________________

Quel *(kel)* (what) **est le numéro de votre téléphone?** ______________________________

Quel est le numéro de téléphone de l'hôtel? ______________________________

Voilà une autre *(oh-truh)* (another) **conversation possible.** *(poh-see-bluh)* Listen to **les mots et comment** they are used.

Thomas: **Allô, c'est Monsieur Cézanne à l'appareil. Je voudrais parler à Madame Villon.**

(a$^{(n)}$-stah$^{(n)}$) *(kee-tay)*
Secrétaire: **Un instant, s'il vous plaît. Ne quittez pas. Excusez-moi, mais la**
one moment — don't hang up — but
(leen-yuh)
ligne est occupée.
busy

Thomas: **Répétez ça, s'il vous plaît. Je parle seulement un peu de français.**
(lah$^{(n)}$t-mah$^{(n)}$)
Parlez plus lentement.
more slowly

Secrétaire: **Excusez-moi, mais la ligne est occupée.**

(oh) (ruh-vwahr)
Thomas: **Oh. Merci. Au revoir.**

(ah$^{(n)}$-kor)
Et encore une autre possibilité.
still

Christine: **Je voudrais des "renseignements" pour Angoulême, s'il vous plaît.**
information
Je voudrais le numéro de téléphone du Docteur Philippe Beauchamp, s'il vous plaît.

Téléphoniste: **Le numéro est 86-45-06.**

Christine: **Répétez le numéro, s'il vous plaît.**

Téléphoniste: **Le numéro est 86-45-06.**

Christine: **Merci beaucoup. Au revoir.**

Téléphoniste: **À votre service. Au revoir.**
you are welcome

Vous êtes maintenant ready to use any **téléphone en France.** Just take it **lentement et** speak clearly.

(noo-blee-ay) *(pah)*
N'oubliez pas that **vous pouvez** ask . . .
don't forget

Combien coûte un appel local? Combien coûte un appel local? ____________

Combien coûte un appel interurbain pour Cannes? ____________

(lay) (zay-tah-zew-nee)
Combien coûte un appel pour les Etats-Unis? ____________
to — the — United States

Combien coûte un appel pour Rome? ____________

N'oubliez pas that **vous avez besoin de la monnaie ou d'un jeton pour le téléphone.**
need

Step 20

Le Métro
(may-tro)
subway

Le métropolitain (may-tro-poh-lee-ta$^{(n)}$), commonly called **"le métro,"** (may-tro) **est le nom pour** the subway. **Le métro à Paris est** the quickest and cheapest form of **transport** (trah$^{(n)}$-spor) [transportation]. It is an extensive **système** (see-stem) which has been expanded by an express line, **le RER** (air-uh-air) **(Réseau Express Régional),** going to **la banlieue** (bah$^{(n)}$-lee-uh) [suburbs] **de** [of] **Paris. A Paris, et dans** smaller **villes** (veel) [cities], **il y a toujours** (too-zhoor) [always] **l'autobus,** a slower but much more scenic means of **transport** (trah$^{(n)}$-spor). **Vous** may also wish to go by **taxi** (tahx-ee). In that case, **trouvez** a taxi station, hail a **taxi** (tahx-ee) on the street or have one called **à votre hôtel. Quels** (kel) [what] **mots sont nécessaires** (nay-say-sair) **pour voyager en métro, en autobus ou en taxi?** Let's learn them by practicing them aloud **et puis** (pwee) by writing them in the blanks **en bas.**

(may-tro) **le métro**	(tahx-ee) **le taxi**	(kahr) **l'autobus/le car**

____________	le taxi	____________

(lah-ray)
l'arrêt = the stop ____________

(leen-yuh)
la ligne = the line ____________

(koh$^{(n)}$-dewk-tur)
le conducteur = the driver le conducteur

(koh$^{(n)}$-troh-lur)
le contrôleur = the ticket-collector ____________

Let's also review **les verbes de transport** at this point.

(moh$^{(n)}$-tay)
monter = to board/to get into ____________

(day-sah$^{(n)}$-druh)
descendre = to get off/to go down descendre

(shah$^{(n)}$-zhay)
changer (d'autobus) = to transfer ____________

(vwhy-ah-zhay)
voyager = to travel ____________

Maps displaying the various **lignes** *(leen-yuh)* **et arrêts** *(ah-ray)* **sont généralement** posted outside every **entrée** *(ah$^{(n)}$-tray)* **de station** *(stah-see-oh$^{(n)}$)* **de métro.** Almost every **plan** *(plah$^{(n)}$)* (map) **de** (of) **Paris** also has a **métro** map included. **Les lignes sont** color-coded to facilitate reading. **Vous achetez les tickets** on entering **la station et vous pouvez acheter un** (one) **ticket ou un carnet** *(kar-nay)* (book) **de dix tickets. Vous** must also decide if **vous** wish **première classe ou deuxième classe.** Check **le nom** of the last **station** on the **ligne** which you should take **et** catch **le train** traveling in that **direction.** *(dee-rek-see-oh$^{(n)}$)* If **vous devez** (must) **changer de train,** look for **les correspondances** *(ko-ray-spoh$^{(n)}$-dah$^{(n)}$s)* (connections, transfers) clearly marked at each **station. Le système d'autobus** works similarly. See **le plan** *(plah$^{(n)}$)* (map) **en bas.**

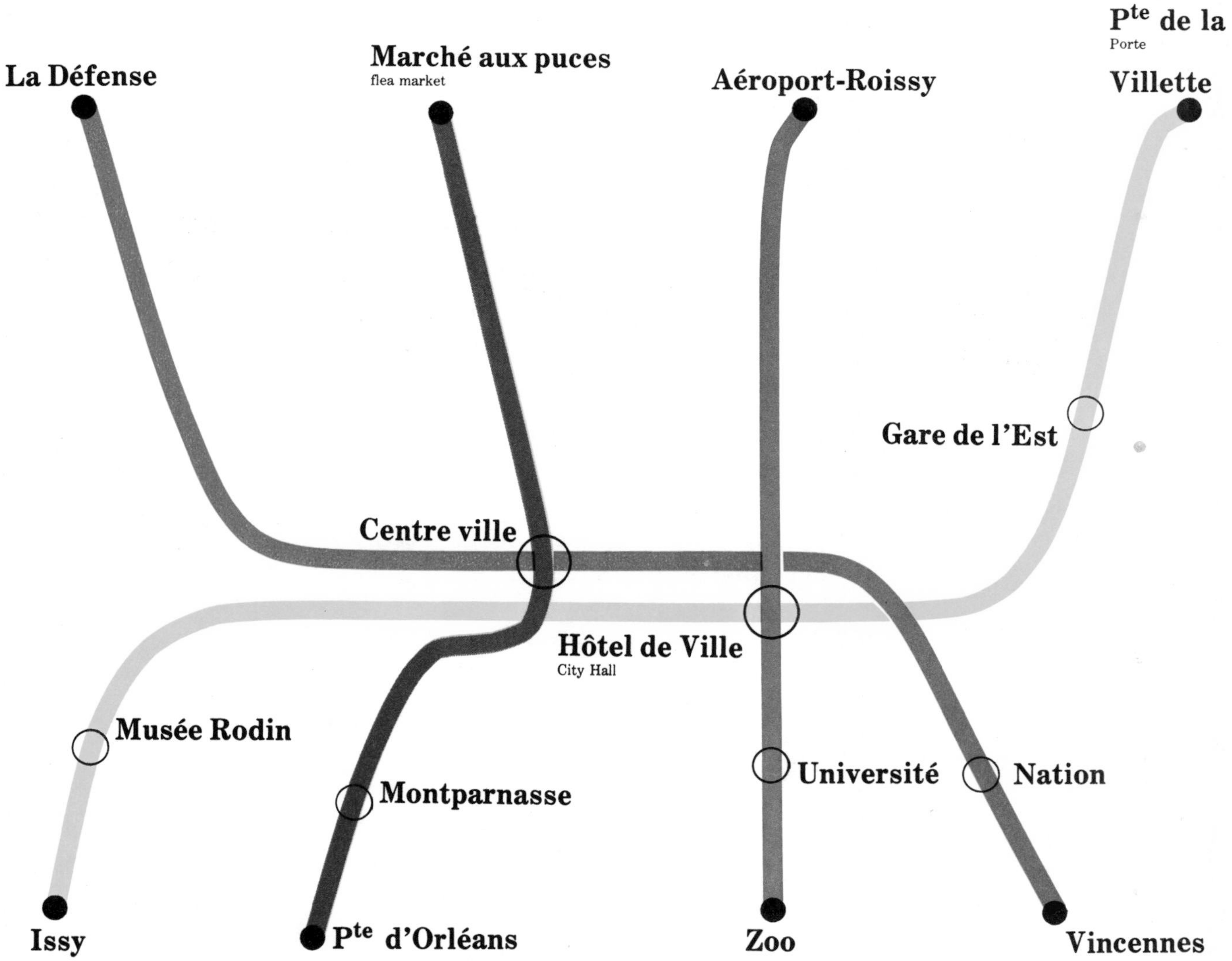

The same basic set of **mots et questions** will see you through traveling **en métro, en car,** (bus) **en auto ou** even **en train.**

Naturally, **la première** *(pruh-mee-air)* **question est "où."**

Où est la station *(stah-see-oh(n))* **de métro** *(may-tro)***?**

Où est l'arrêt *(lah-ray)* **d'autobus?**

Où est la station de taxis?

Où est la tête *(tet)* (head) **de taxis?**

Practice the following basic **questions** out loud **et puis** write them in the blanks **à droite.**

1. **Où est la station de métro?** ____________________

   Où est l'arrêt d'autobus? Où est l'arrêt d'autobus?

   Où est la station de taxis? ____________________

2. **Quelle est la fréquence** *(fray-kah(n)s)* (frequency) **des** *(day)* **trains pour le Louvre?** ____________________

   Quelle est la fréquence des autobus pour Montparnasse? ____________________

   Quelle est la fréquence des taxis pour l'aéroport? ____________________

3. **Quand** *(kah(n))* (when) **le train part-il?** ____________________

   Quand l'autobus part-il? ____________________

   Quand le taxi part-il? ____________________

4. **Quand le train pour Roissy** *(rwah-see)* **part-il?** ____________________

   Quand l'autobus pour Roissy part-il? ____________________

   Quand le taxi pour Roissy part-il? ____________________

5. **Combien coûte un ticket de métro?** ____________________

   Combien coûte un ticket d'autobus? ____________________

   Le tarif c'est combien? Le tarif c'est combien?

   Combien est-ce que je vous (to you) **dois** *(dwah)* (owe)**?** ____________________

Maintenant that **vous avez** gotten into the swing of things, practice the following patterns aloud, substituting **"autobus"** for **"métro" et** so on.

1. **Où est-ce** *(ess)* **qu'on** *(koh(n))* **achète** *(nah-shet)* **un ticket de métro? d'autobus? de train?**

2. **Quand part le train pour La Défense? pour le centre ville? pour Montparnasse? pour l'Hôtel de Ville? pour l'aéroport Roissy** *(rwah-see)* **? pour la gare? pour la Tour Eiffel?**

3. **Où est la station de métro pour aller** (to go) **à l'aéroport?**

   Où est l'arrêt *(lah-ray)* **d'autobus pour aller à la Tour** *(toor)* **Eiffel** *(ay-fell)* **?**

   Où est la station de métro pour aller au *(oh)* **centre** *(sah(n)-truh)* **ville** *(veel)* **?**

   Où est l'arrêt d'autobus pour aller au Zoo *(zoh)* **?**

   Où est la station de métro pour aller au Musée *(mew-zay)* **Rodin** *(ro-da(n))* **?**

   Où est l'arrêt d'autobus pour aller à la gare de l'Est *(lest)* **?**

   Où est la station de métro pour aller à l'université?

   Où est l'arrêt d'autobus pour aller au marché aux puces?

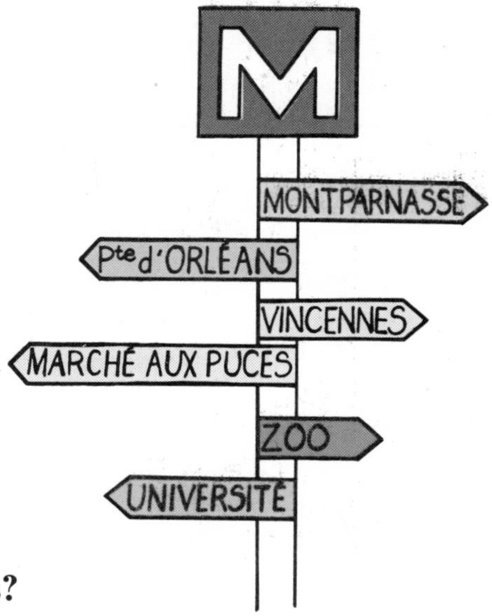

Lisez la conversation suivante, très typique *(tee-peek)* **, et écrivez-** *(ay-kree-vay)* **la** *(lah)* (it) in the blanks **à droite.**

Quelle *(kel)* (which) **ligne va** *(vah)* (goes) **à Vincennes** *(va(n)-sen)* **?** ______________________

La ligne rouge va à Vincennes. ______________________

A quelle fréquence? ______________________

Toutes *(toot)* (every) **les dix minutes.** Toutes les dix minutes.

Dois-je *(dwah-zh)* (must I) **changer de train?** ______________________

Oui, au centre ville. Vous avez une correspondance *(ko-ray-spoh(n)-dah(n)s)* (connection) **à la station "Centre ville."**

Oui, au centre ville.

Il *(eel)* **faut** *(foh)* (it is necessary) **combien de temps d'ici** (from here) **à Vincennes?** ______________________

Il *(eel)* **faut** *(foh)* **20 minutes.** ______________________

Combien coûte le ticket pour Vincennes? ______________________

Un franc cinquante. ______________________

Pouvez-vous translate the following thoughts **en français? Les réponses sont en bas.**

1. Where is the subway stop? ____________________
2. What costs a ticket to City Hall? ____________________
3. How often do the buses go to the airport? ____________________
4. Where does one buy a subway ticket? ____________________
5. Where is the bus stop? Où est l'arrêt d'autobus?
6. I would like to get out. ____________________
7. Must I transfer? ____________________
8. Where must I transfer? ____________________

Voilà encore trois verbes.

(lah-vay) **laver** = to wash	*(pear-druh)* **perdre** = to lose	*(eel)(foh)* **il faut** = it is necessary
laver	____________	____________

You know the basic "plug-in" formula, so translate the following thoughts **avec ces nouveaux verbes. Les réponses sont aussi en bas.**

1. I wash the jacket. ____________________
2. You lose the book. ____________________
3. It takes (is necessary) 20 minutes to go to Vincennes. ____________________
4. It takes three hours by car. ____________________

RÉPONSES

1. **Où est la station de métro?**
2. **Combien coûte un ticket pour l'Hôtel de Ville?**
3. **Quelle est la fréquence des autobus pour l'aéroport?**
4. **Où est-ce qu'on achète un ticket de métro?**
5. **Où est l'arrêt d'autobus?**
6. **Je voudrais descendre.**
7. **Dois-je changer?**
8. **Où dois-je changer?**

---

1. **Je lave la jaquette.**
2. **Vous perdez le livre.**
3. **Il faut vingt minutes pour aller à Vincennes.**
4. **Il faut trois heures en voiture (en auto).**

La Vente et l'Achat

(vah(n)t) (lah-shah)
selling buying

Shopping abroad **est** exciting. The simple everyday task of buying **un litre de lait ou une** (pohm) **pomme** (apple) becomes a challenge that **vous** should **maintenant** be able to meet quickly **et** easily. Of course, **vous** will purchase **des** (soo-vuh-neer) **souvenirs** (souvenirs)**, des timbres-poste et des cartes postales,** but **n'oubliez pas** those many other **choses** ranging from shoelaces to (ah-spee-reen) **aspirine** (aspirin) that **vous** might need unexpectedly. **Savez-vous** (know) **la différence entre une** (lee-brair-ree) **librairie** (bookstore) **et une** (boo-shuh-ree) **boucherie** (butcher shop)? **Non.** Let's learn about the different (boo-teek) **boutiques** (shops) **et** (ma-gah-za(n)) **magasins** (stores) **en France.**

En bas il y a un (plah(n)) **plan** (map) **d'une** (sek-see-oh(n)) **section de Paris.**

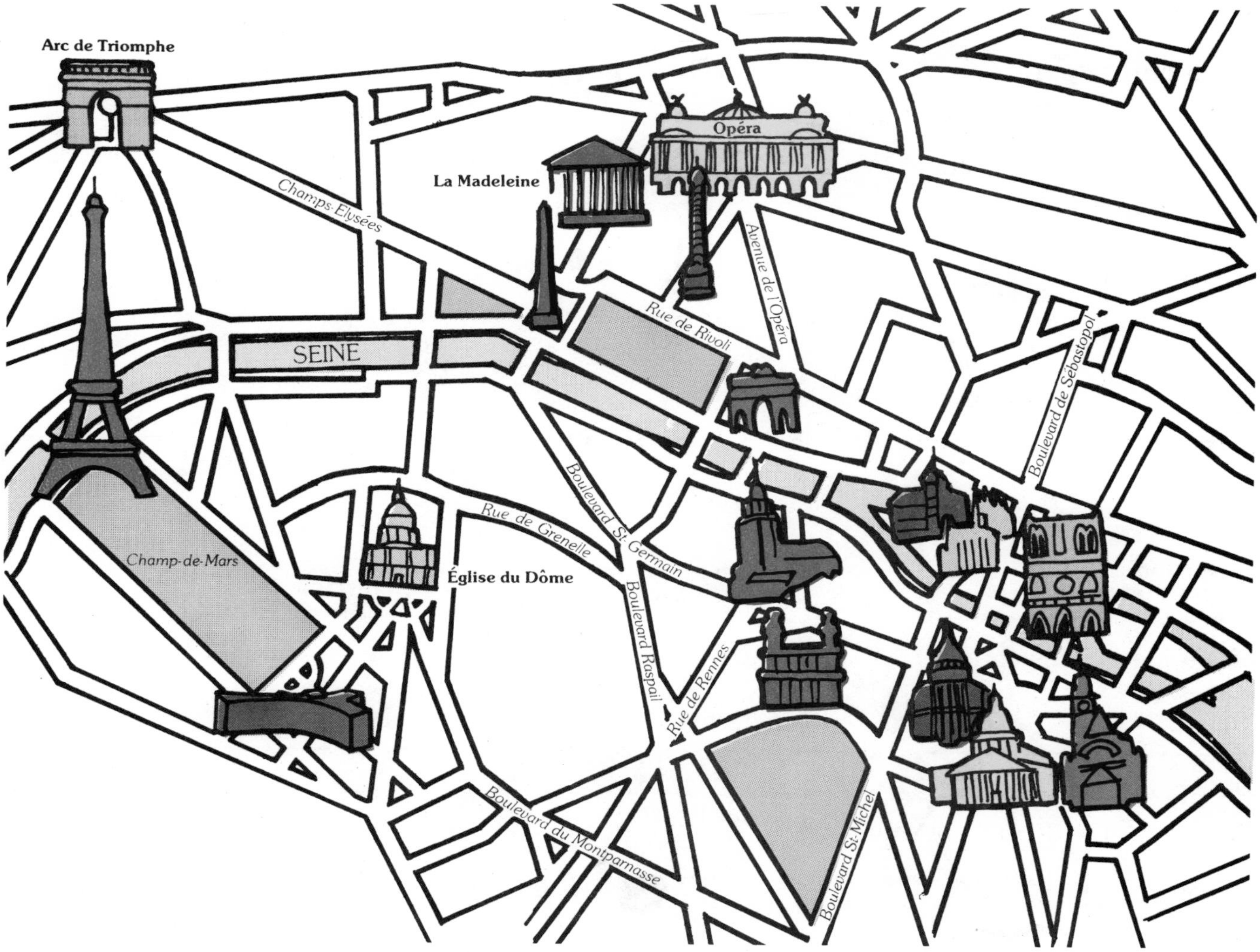

Sur les pages suivantes il y a all types of (ma-gah-za(n)) **magasins en France.** Be sure to fill in the blanks **sous les images avec le nom du magasin.**

la boulangerie, *(boo-lah(n)-zhuh-ree)* bakery
où on achète le pain *(oh(n)) (nah-shet)*

la boucherie, *(boo-shuh-ree)* butcher shop
où on achète la viande *(vee-ah(n)nd)* meat

la blanchisserie, *(blah(n)-shee-suh-ree)* laundry
où on lave les vêtements washes *(vet-mah(n))* clothes

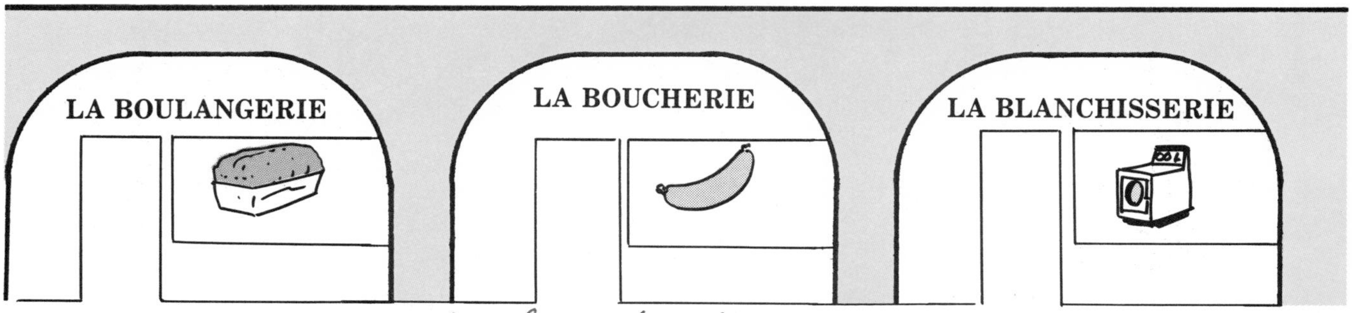

______ la boucherie ______ ______

le café,
où on boit le café *(bwah)*

la quincaillerie, *(ka(n)-ky-yuh-ree)* hardware store
où on achète la pile *(peel)* battery

la pharmacie, *(far-mah-see)*
où on achète l'aspirine *(lah-spee-reen)*

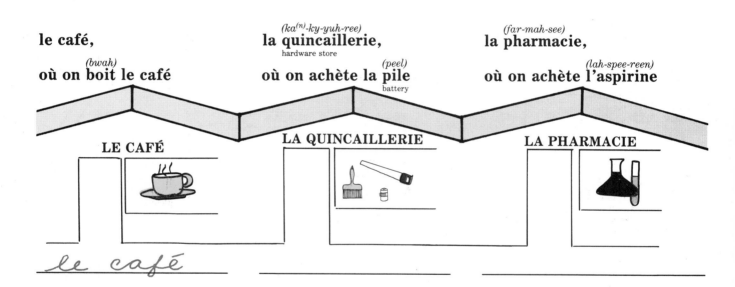

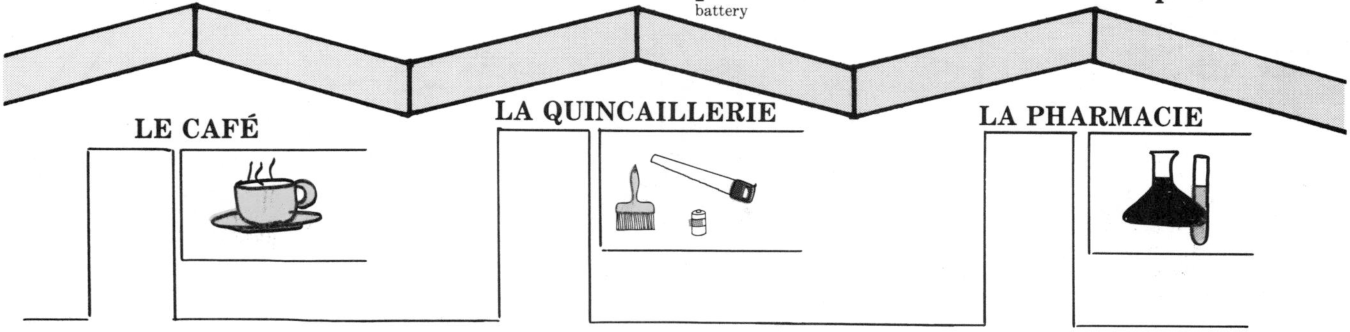

le café ______ ______ ______

le fleuriste, *(flur-east)* florist
où on achète les fleurs

le bureau de tabac, *(tah-bah)* tobacco store
où on achète le tabac tobacco
et les cigarettes *(see-gah-ret)*

la confiserie, *(koh(n)-fee-suh-ree)* confectionery
où on achète les bonbons *(boh(n)-boh(n))*
et le chocolat *(show-ko-lah)*

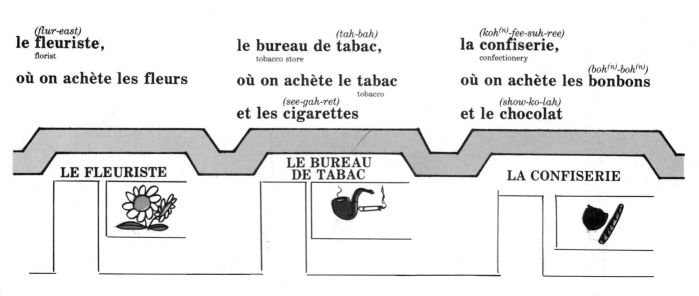

______ ______ ______

la laiterie/la crémerie, *(lay-tuh-ree) (kray-muh-ree)* — dairy

où on achète le lait

la pâtisserie, *(pah-tee-suh-ree)* — pastry shop

où on achète les pâtisseries — pastries

le marchand de légumes, *(mar-shah(n)) (lay-gewm)* — seller, vegetables

où on achète les légumes

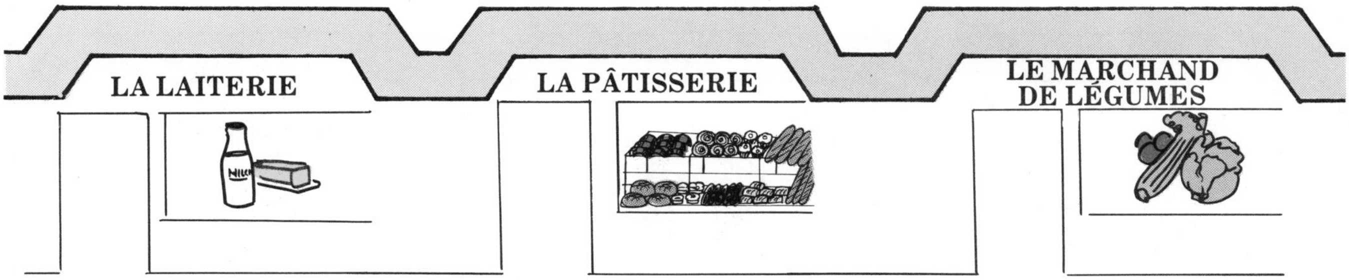

______________________ ______________________ ______________________

le parking *(par-keeng)* — parking lot

où on gare l'auto *(gar)* — park

le coiffeur, *(kwah-fur)* — hairdresser

où on coupe les cheveux *(koop) (shuh-vuh)* — cuts, hair

le tailleur, *(tie-yur)* — tailor

où on fait les vêtements *(vet-mah(n))* — makes

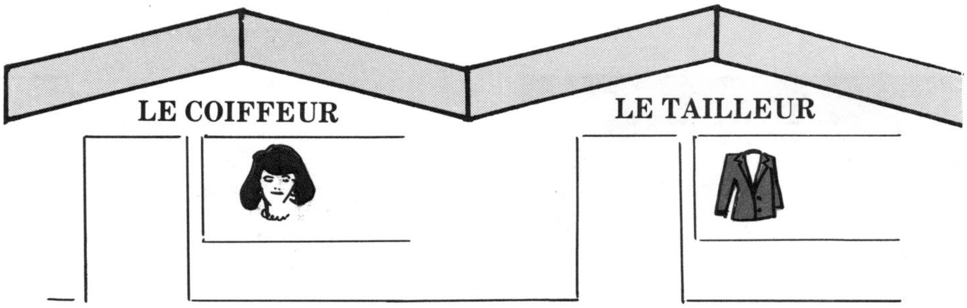

______________________ ______________________ *le tailleur*

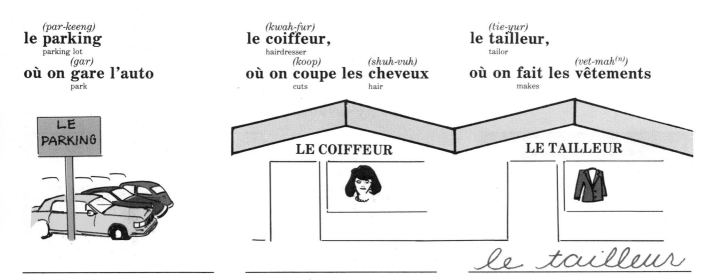

le bureau de poste, — post office

où on achète les timbres

le commissariat de police, *(ko-mee-sah-ree-ah)* — police station

où on trouve la police *(poh-lease)*

la banque,

où on change l'argent et touche le chèque *(shah(n)zh) (toosh) (shek)* — exchanges, cashes

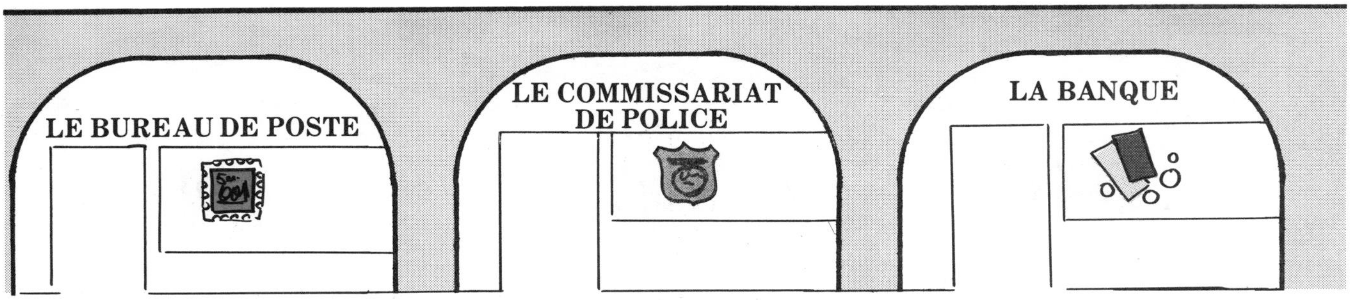

______________________ ______________________ ______________________

(lay-pee-suh-ree)
l'épicerie,
grocery store

où on achète la viande,

les fruits et le lait

(shar-kew-tuh-ree)
la charcuterie,
delicatessen

(soh-see-soh^(n))
où on achète le saucisson
salami/sausage

(soh-sees)
et la saucisse

(fwee-tee-ay)
le fruitier,
fruit vendor

où on achète les fruits

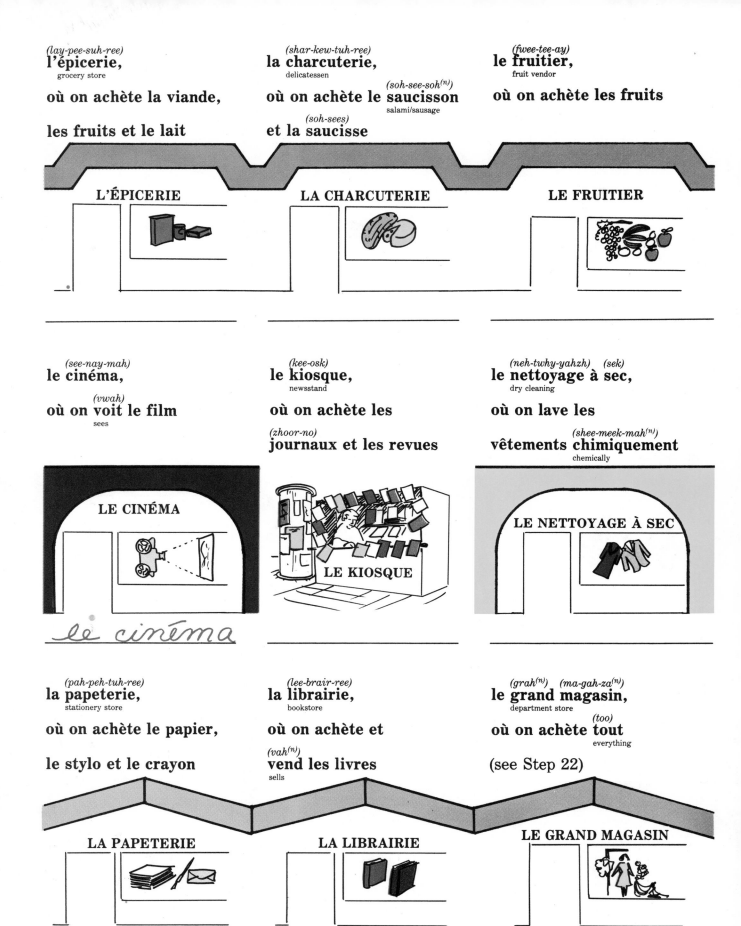

(see-nay-mah)
le cinéma,

(vwah)
où on voit le film
sees

(kee-osk)
le kiosque,
newsstand

où on achète les

(zhoor-no)
journaux et les revues

(neh-twhy-yahzh) (sek)
le nettoyage à sec,
dry cleaning

où on lave les

(shee-meek-mah^(n))
vêtements chimiquement
chemically

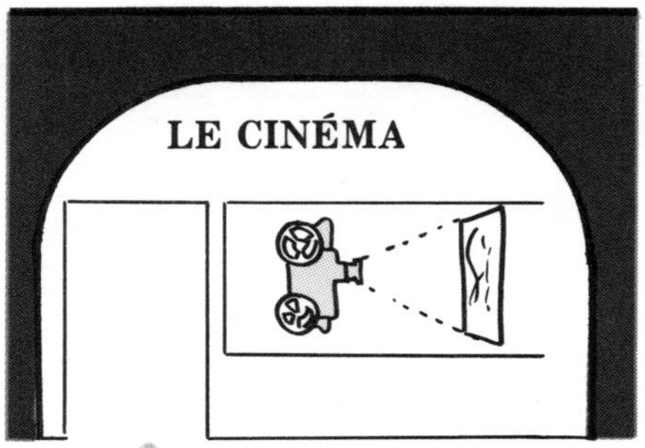

le cinéma

(pah-peh-tuh-ree)
la papeterie,
stationery store

où on achète le papier,

le stylo et le crayon

(lee-brair-ree)
la librairie,
bookstore

où on achète et

(vah^(n))
vend les livres
sells

(grah^(n)) (ma-gah-za^(n))
le grand magasin,
department store

(too)
où on achète tout
everything

(see Step 22)

(mar-shay)
le marché, où on (market)
achète les légumes et fruits

(sue-pear-mar-shay)
le supermarché,
où on achète tout (everything)

(stah-see-oh$^{(n)}$)(day-sah$^{(n)}$s)
la station d'essence, (gas station)
où on achète l'essence

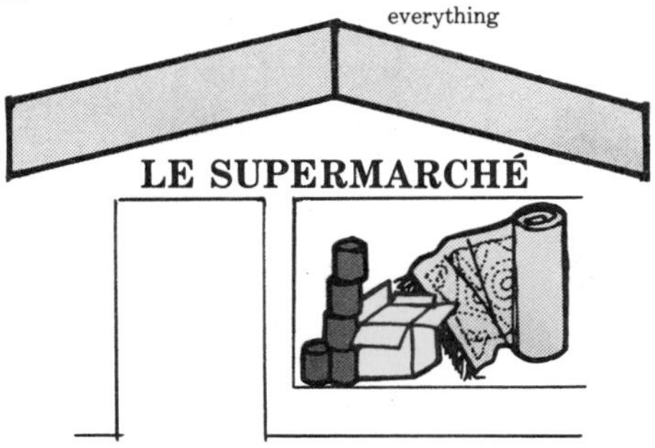

_______________ *le supermarché* _______________

(lah-zhah$^{(n)}$s) (vwhy-ahzh)
l'agence de voyage, (travel agency)
où on achète les
billets d'avion

(lor-low-zhuh-ree)
l'horlogerie, (clock and watchmaker's shop)
où on achète les horloges

(pwah-soh$^{(n)}$-nuh-ree)
la poissonnerie (fish market)
(pwah-soh$^{(n)}$)
où on achète le poisson (fish)

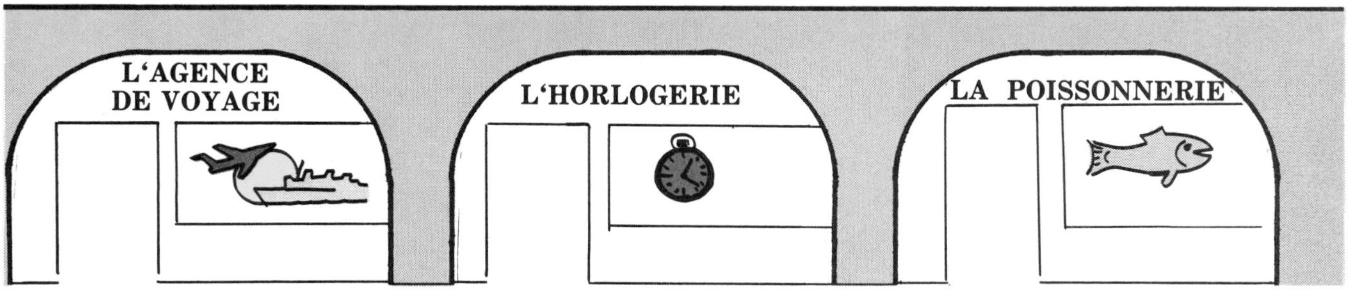

_______________ _______________ _______________

Quand les magasins français sont-ils ouverts? (are they open; ouverts = oo-vair) **Les magasins français sont généralement ouverts de lundi à samedi, de 9:00 à 18:30. Beaucoup de petits magasins** will close over the lunch hour **(12:00 — 14:00),** although this is increasingly less true **à Paris.** Some foodshops **sont ouverts le dimanche,** (on Sundays) **et** it is often a family ritual to make a trip **à la boulangerie où pâtisserie** to pick up **le pain et** special weekend **gâteau** (gah-toe) (cake). Many shops **sont aussi** (toh-see) (also) closed **le lundi.** Local, open-air **marchés sont** truly **une expérience,** (ek-spay-ree-ah$^{(n)}$s) so be sure to check **les heures** (lay) (zuhr) of the one closest to **votre hôtel.**

Y a-t-il (ee) (ah-teel) (is there) anything else which makes **les magasins français différents** from **les magasins américains? Oui.** Look at **les images à la prochaine page.**

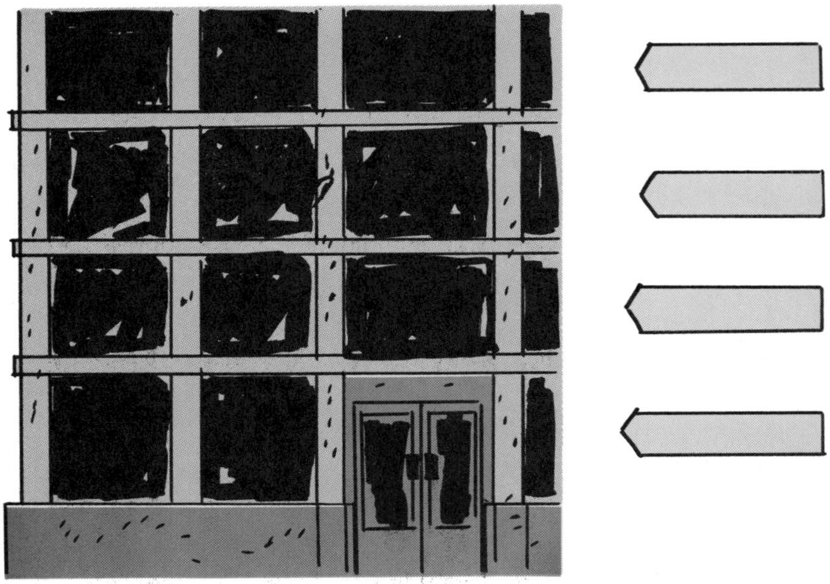

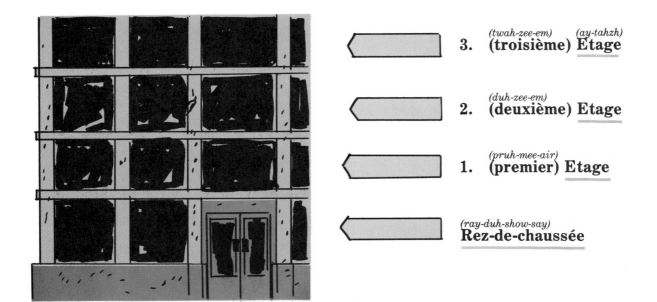

3. *(twah-zee-em)* **(troisième)** *(ay-tahzh)* **Etage**

2. *(duh-zee-em)* **(deuxième) Etage**

1. *(pruh-mee-air)* **(premier) Etage**

(ray-duh-show-say) **Rez-de-chaussée**

En France the ground floor **s'appelle** *(ray-duh-show-say)* **"le rez-de-chaussée."** The first floor **est** the next floor up **et** so on. Now that **vous** know **les noms pour les magasins français,** let's practice shopping.

I. First step — **Où?**

Où est la laiterie? **Où est la banque?** **Où est le cinéma?**

Go through **les magasins** introduced in this Step **et** ask, **"Où"** **avec** *(shahk)* **chaque** (each) **magasin.** Another way of asking **où** is to ask

(ee)(ah-teel) **Y a-t-il une laiterie** *(pray)* **près** (near) *(dee-see)* **d'ici** (here)**?**

Y a-t-il une banque près d'ici?

Go through **les magasins** again using **cette** (this) **nouvelle question.**

II. Next step — tell them what **vous** are looking for, need **ou voudriez!**

1) **J'ai besoin de . . .** J'ai besoin de ____________

2) **Avez-vous . . . ?** ____________

3) **Je voudrais . . .** ____________

J'ai besoin d'un crayon.

Avez-vous un crayon?

Je voudrais un crayon.

J'ai besoin d'un kilo de pommes. *(pohm)*

Avez-vous un kilo de pommes?

Je voudrais un kilo de pommes.

Go through the glossary at the end of **ce livre et** select **vingt mots.** Drill the above patterns **avec ces vingt mots.** Don't cheat. Drill them **aujourd'hui. Maintenant,** take **encore** (more) **vingt mots de votre** glossary **et** do the same.

III. Next step — find out **combien ça coûte.**

1) **Combien est-ce?** *(ess)* ____________________

2) **Combien est-ce que ça coûte?** *(kuh) (sah)* ____________________

Combien coûte le crayon? *(koot)*

Combien coûte la carte-postale? *(koot)*

Combien coûte le timbre?

Combien coûte un kilo de pommes?

Combien coûte un kilo d'oranges?

Combien coûte un kilo de viande?

Using these same **mots** that **vous** selected **en haut,** drill **ces questions aussi.**

IV. If **vous ne savez pas où trouver** something, **vous demandez** *(duh-mah(n)-day)* (ask)

Où est-ce qu'on achète de l'aspirine? *(lah-spee-reen)*

Où est-ce qu'on achète des lunettes de soleil? *(lew-net) (so-lay)*

Once **vous trouvez** what **vous** would like, **vous dites, Je voudrais ça, s'il vous plaît.**

Ou, if **vous** would not like it, **Je ne voudrais pas ça, merci.**

Vous êtes maintenant all set to shop for anything!

Step 22

Le Grand Magasin
(grah(n)) (ma-gah-za(n))
department store

At this point, **vous** should just about be ready for **votre voyage en France. Vous** have gone shopping for those last-minute odds 'n ends. Most likely, the store directory at your local **grand magasin** did not look like the one **en bas. Vous** know already **beaucoup de mots et vous pouvez** guess at **beaucoup d'autres** (doh-truh) (others). **Vous savez** (know) **qu'** (that) **"enfant" est français pour** "child," so if **vous avez besoin de** something **pour un enfant, vous** would probably look on the **deuxième** (duh-zee-em) **ou troisième** (twah-zee-em) **étage** (ay-tahzh), **n'est-ce pas?**

6ME ÉTAGE	**boulangerie** **caféteria** **charcuterie** **alcool**	**volaille** **alimentation** **fruits** **légumes**	**produits congelés** **vin** **gibier** **viande**
5ME ÉTAGE	**lits** **linge** **miroirs**	**ameublement** **lampes** **tapis**	**tableaux** **électroménager**
4ME ÉTAGE	**vaisselle** **cristal**	**service de table** **ameublement de cuisine**	**clés** **faïence** **porcelaine**
3ME ÉTAGE	**livres** **télévisions** **meubles d'enfant** **jouets**	**radios** **instruments de musique** **papeterie** **disques**	**tabac** **restaurant** **journaux** **revues**
2ME ÉTAGE	**tout pour l'enfant** **vêtements de femme** **chapeaux de femme**	**vêtements d'homme** **chaussures d'enfant** **photo**	**toilettes** **antiquités**
1ER ÉTAGE	**accessoires d'auto** **lingerie** **mouchoirs**	**maillots de bain** **chaussures de femme** **chaussures d'homme**	**équipement de sport** **outils** **mobilier de camping**
R	**parapluies** **cartes** **chapeaux d'homme** **bijouterie**	**gants** **maroquinerie** **chaussettes** **ceintures**	**pendules/montres** **parfumerie** **confiserie**

Let's start a check **liste** (least) **pour votre voyage.** Besides **vêtements** (vet-mah(n)), **de quoi** (kwah) (what) **avez-vous besoin? Qu'est-ce** (kess) (what) **qu'il** (keel) **faut** (is necessary) **en Europe?**

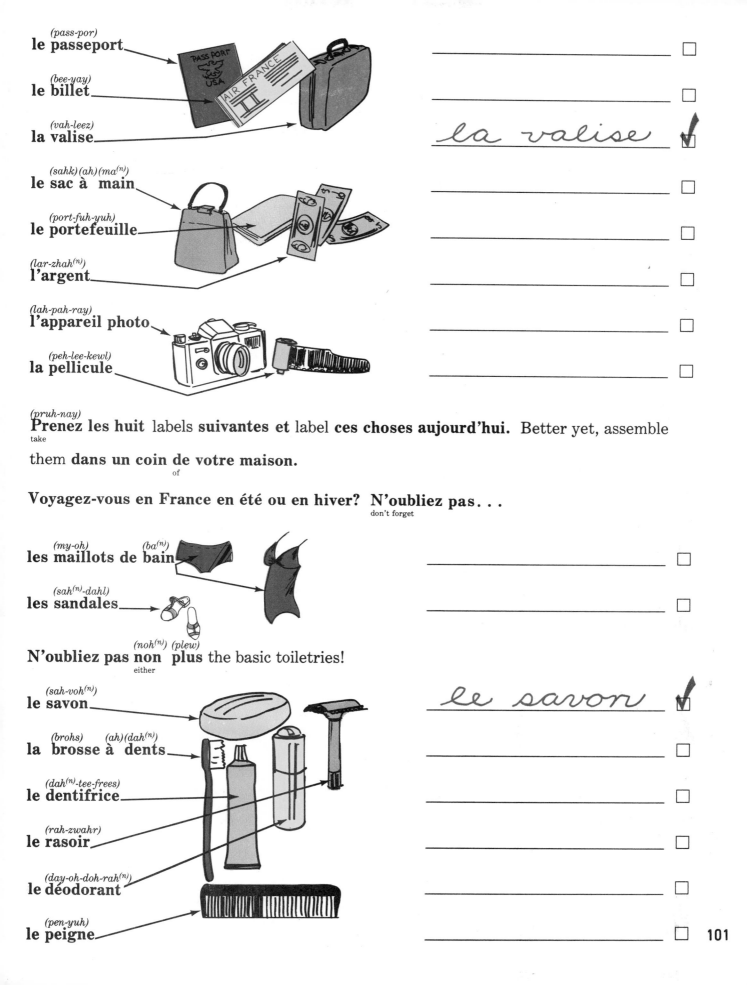

(pass-por)
le passeport ______________ ☐

(bee-yay)
le billet ______________ ☐

(vah-leez)
la valise ___la valise___ ☑

(sahk) (ah) (ma$^{(n)}$)
le sac à main ______________ ☐

(port-fuh-yuh)
le portefeuille ______________ ☐

(lar-zhah$^{(n)}$)
l'argent ______________ ☐

(lah-pah-ray)
l'appareil photo ______________ ☐

(peh-lee-kewl)
la pellicule ______________ ☐

(pruh-nay)
Prenez (take) **les huit** labels **suivantes et** label **ces choses aujourd'hui.** Better yet, assemble them **dans un coin de** (of) **votre maison.**

Voyagez-vous en France en été ou en hiver? N'oubliez pas (don't forget) **. . .**

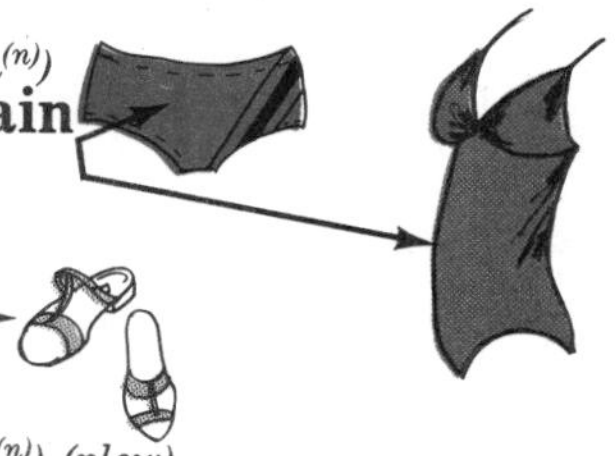

(my-oh) (ba$^{(n)}$)
les maillots de bain ______________ ☐

(sah$^{(n)}$-dahl)
les sandales ______________ ☐

(noh$^{(n)}$) (plew)
N'oubliez pas non plus (either) the basic toiletries!

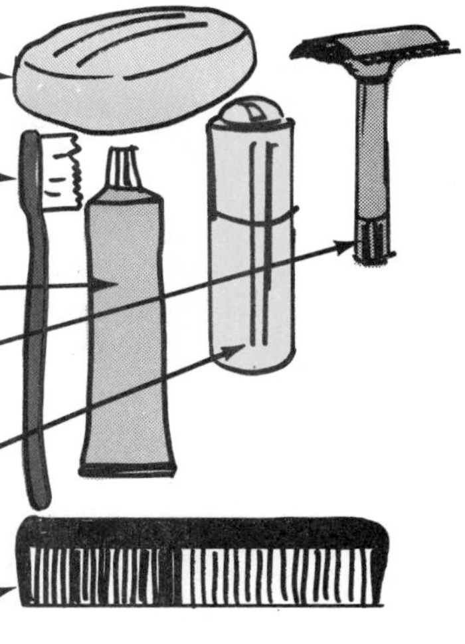

(sah-voh$^{(n)}$)
le savon ___le savon___ ☑

(brohs) (ah) (dah$^{(n)}$)
la brosse à dents ______________ ☐

(dah$^{(n)}$-tee-frees)
le dentifrice ______________ ☐

(rah-zwahr)
le rasoir ______________ ☐

(day-oh-doh-rah$^{(n)}$)
le déodorant ______________ ☐

(pen-yuh)
le peigne ______________ ☐

For the rest of the **choses**, let's start **avec** the outside layers **et** work our way in.

(mah(n)-toe)
le manteau ______________ ☑

(la(n)-pear-may-ah-bluh)
l'imperméable ______________ ☐

(pah-rah-plew-ee)
le parapluie ______________ ☐

(gah(n))
les gants ______________ ☐

(shah-poh)
le chapeau ______________ ☐

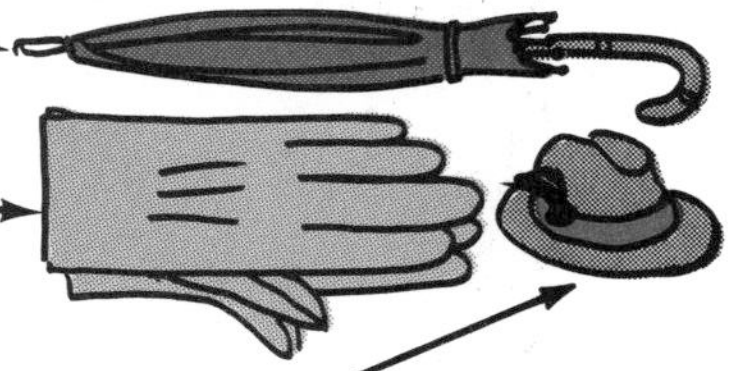

(boat)
la botte la botte ☐

(show-sewr)
la chaussure ______________ ☐

(show-set)
la chaussette ______________ ☑

(bas)
les bas ______________ ☐

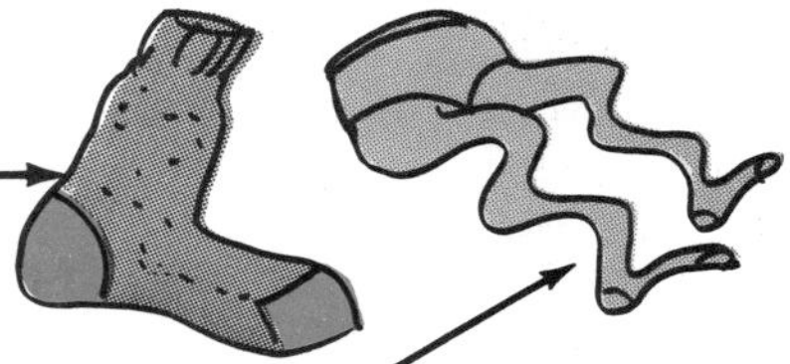

Prenez *(pruh-nay)* [take] **les quinze** labels **suivantes et** label **ces choses.** Check **et** make sure that **elles sont propres** *(proh-pruh)* [clean] **et** ready **pour votre voyage.** Be sure to do the same **avec le reste** *(rehst)* [rest] **des** [of the] **choses** that **vous** pack. Check them off on **cette liste** as **vous** organize them. From now on, **vous avez du "dentifrice" et non pas** [not] "toothpaste."

(pee-zhah-mah)
le pyjama le pyjama ☐

(shuh-meez) (nwee)
la chemise de nuit ______________ ☐

(rohb) (shah(n)-bruh)
la robe de chambre ______________ ☐

(pah(n)-too-fluh)
les pantoufles ______________ ☐

La robe de chambre et les pantoufles peuvent *(puhv)* [can] **aussi** double **pour vous à la plage.** *(plahzh)* [beach]

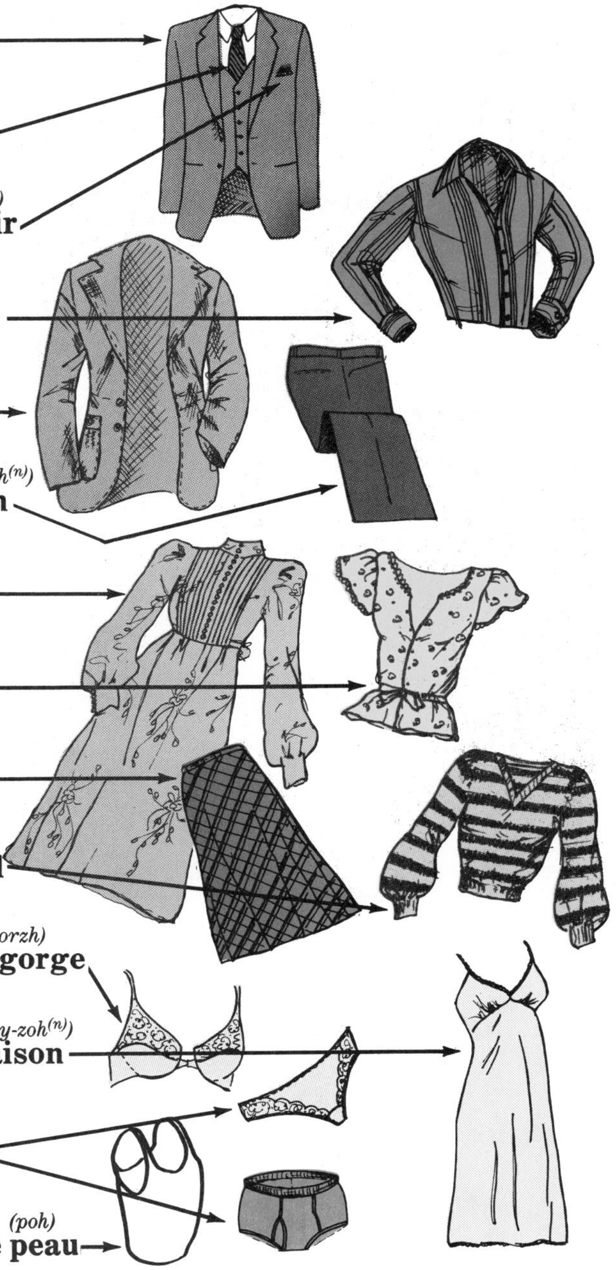

(koh(n)-play) **le complet**	____________	☐
(krah-vaht) **la cravate**	____________	☐
(moo-shwahr) **le mouchoir**	____________	☐
(shuh-meez) **la chemise**	____________	☐
(veh-stoh(n)) **le veston**	____________	☐
(pah(n)-tah-loh(n)) **le pantalon**	____________	☑
(rohb) **la robe**	____________	☐
(blooz) **la blouse**	la blouse	☐
(zheewp) **la jupe**	____________	☐
(shah(n)-dye) **le chandail**	____________	☐
(soo-tee-a(n)-gorzh) **le soutien-gorge**	____________	☐
(koh(n)-bee-nay-zoh(n)) **la combinaison**	____________	☐
(sleep) **les slips**	____________	☐
(tree-ko) (poh) **le tricot de peau**	____________	☐

Having assembled **ces choses, vous êtes préparé** *(pray-pah-ray)* [prepared] **pour votre voyage.** However, being human means occasionally forgetting something. Look again at **le grand magasin** directory.

À quel étage trouvez-vous . . . [on which]

vêtements d'homme? **Au** 2.me **étage.**

un chapeau pour une dame? **Au** ____________ **étage.**

livres? **Au** ____________ **étage.**

lingerie? **Au** ____________ **étage.**

cristal? Au ______________ étage.

parfum? Au ______________.

vêtements de femme? Au ______________ étage.

Maintenant, just remember your basic **questions. Répétez la conversation typique** *(tee-peek)* **en bas** out loud **et puis** by filling in the blanks.

Où est-ce qu'on trouve les pantalons de femme? ______________

Dans le rayon *(ray-oh$^{(n)}$)* [department] **de vêtements de femme.** ______________

Où est le rayon de vêtements de femme? ______________

Au deuxième étage. Au deuxième étage.

Où est-ce qu'on trouve le savon et le dentifrice? ______________

Au rez-de-chaussée. ______________

Aussi, n'oubliez pas de demander *(duh-mah$^{(n)}$-day)* [ask] **. . .**

Où est l'ascenseur? *(lah-sah$^{(n)}$-sur)* [elevator] ______________

Où est l'escalier? *(leh-skah-lee-ay)* [steps] ______________

Où est l'escalier roulant? *(leh-skah-lee-ay) (roo-lah$^{(n)}$)* [escalator] ______________

Whether **vous avez besoin d'un pantalon de femme ou d'une chemise d'homme, les mots nécessaires sont** the same.

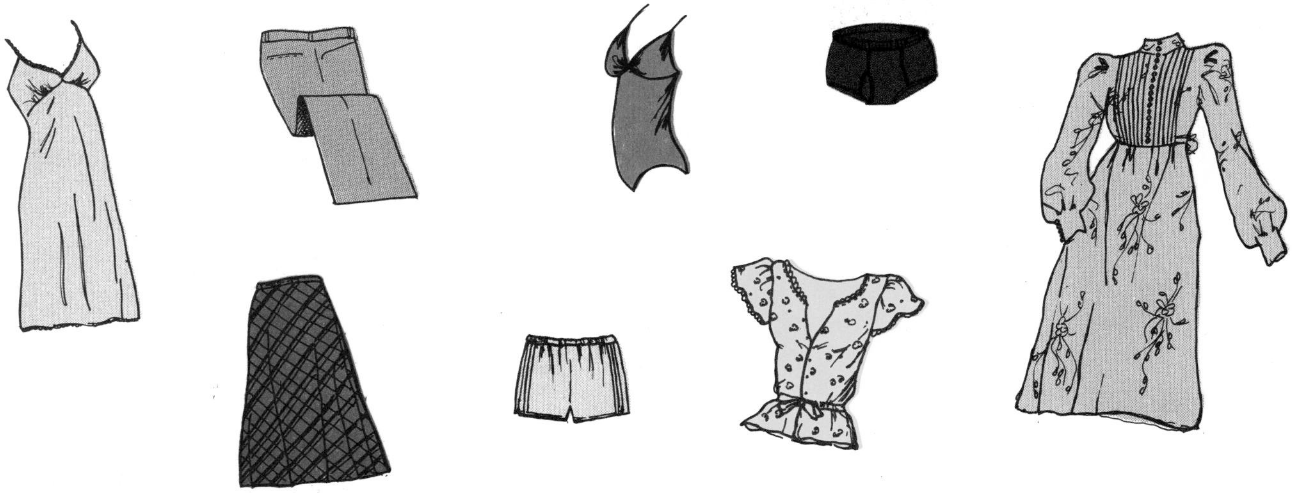

(tie)
Quelle taille?
size

____

(pwa$^{(n)}$-tewr)
Quelle pointure?
size for shoes and gloves

____

(muh) (vah)
Ça me va.
me fits

Ça me va.

(nuh) (muh) (vah) (pah)
Ça ne me va pas.
doesn't fit

____

(prah$^{(n)}$) (sah)
Je prends ça.
take that

____

Combien est-ce?

____

C'est tout, merci beaucoup.
that's all

____

Clothing Sizes: **FEMMES**

chaussures									
American	5	5½	6	6½	7	7½	8	8½	9
Continental	35	35	36	37	38	38	38	39	40

vêtements						
American	8	10	12	14	16	18
Continental	36	38	40	42	44	46

blouses,chandails							
American	32	34	36	38	40	42	44
Continental	40	42	44	46	48	50	52

Clothing Sizes: **HOMMES**

chaussures										
American	7	7½	8	8½	9	9½	10	10½	11	11½
Continental	39	40	41	42	43	43	44	44	45	45

vêtements								
American	34	36	38	40	42	44	46	48
Continental	44	46	48	50	52	54	56	58

chemises								
American	14	14½	15	15½	16	16½	17	17½
Continental	36	37	38	39	40	41	42	43

(pray-pah-ray)
Maintenant, vous êtes préparé pour votre voyage. Vous savez tout that you need.

The next step will give you a quick review of international road signs **et** then **vous** are off to **l'aéroport. Bon voyage! Amusez-vous bien!**

Step 23

= **Dangerous Intersection**

Voilà some of the most important **signalisations** (seen-yal-ee-zah-see-oh(n)) [signs] **routières** (roo-tee-air) [road] **internationales.** (a(n)-tair-nah-see-oh(n)-nahl) [international] Remember that **en France** a basic rule of the road is **priorité** (pree-oh-ree-tay) [yield] **à droite.** [to the right] **Conduisez** (koh(n)-dwee-zay) [drive] **prudemment!** (prew-duh-mah(n)) [carefully]

Bon voyage!

Danger

Dangerous curve

Dangerous intersection

Closed to all vehicles

Prohibited for motor vehicles

Prohibited for motor vehicles on Sundays and holidays

No entry

Stop

Main road ahead, yield the right of way

You have the right of way

Additional sign indicating the right of way

One-way street

Dead-end street

Detour

Traffic circle

No left turn

No U-turn

No parking

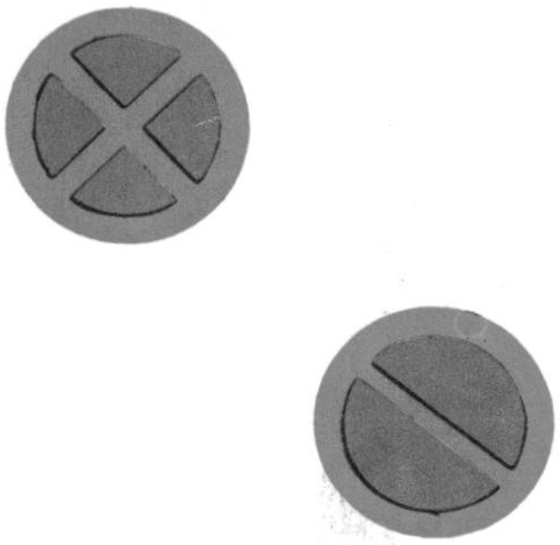

No parking or waiting

No passing

Speed limit

End of speed limit

Beginning of **autoroute**

Railroad crossing
240 meters

Railroad crossing
160 meters

Railroad crossing
80 meters

Customs

Federal Highway
Number

City limit

End of city limit

Parking permitted

Road ends, water
ahead

GLOSSARY

A

a/avoir ... has/to have
à ... at, to, in
à côté de ... next to
à demain ... till tomorrow
à droite ... to the right
à gauche ... to the left
accident, le ... accident
acheter ... to buy
addition, la ... bill in a restaurant
adresse, la ... address
aéroport, le ... airport
Afrique, la ... Africa
Afrique du sud, la ... South Africa
agence de location, la ... car rental agency
agence de voyage, la ... travel agency
ai/avoir ... have/to have
aidez-moi ... help me! aid me!
AJ, la ... youth hostel
alcool, le ... alcohol
Allemagne, la ... Germany
Allemange de l'est, la ... East Germany
Allemagne d l'ouest, la ... West Germany
aller ... to go,one way
aller et retour ... round trip
américain (e) ... American
Amérique, la ... America
ameublement, le ... furnishings
amusez-vous ... amuse yourself
an, le ... year
ananas, le ... pineapple
anglais (e) ... English
Angleterre, la ... England
animal, le ... animal
année, la ... year
annuaire, le ... telephone book
août, le ... August
appareil, le ... gadget, appliance
appartement, le ... apartment
s'appeler ... to be called
appel de téléphone, le ... telephone call
appétit, le ... appetite
apprendre ... to learn
approximativement ... approximately
après-midi, le ... afternoon
arbre, le ... tree
argent, le ... money
armoire, la ... closet, wardrobe
arrêt, le ... stop, arrest
arrivée, la ... arrival
arriver ... to arrive
ascenseur, le ... elevator
assiette, la ... plate
assis (e) ... seated
attendre ... to wait for
atterrir ... to land
au ... in the, at the
auberge, la ... country inn
auberge de la jeunesse, la ... youth hostel
au coin ... on the corner
au milieu ... in the middle
au revoir ... goodbye
au-dessus de ... over
aujourd'hui ... today
aussi ... also
auto, la ... car
autobus, le ... bus
automobile à louer, la ... rental car
automne, le ... Autumn
autoroute, la ... freeway
autre ... another
avec ... with
avez/avoir ... have/to have
avion, le ... airplane
avoir ... to have
avoir besoin de ... to need
avons/avoir ... have/to have
avril ... April

B

baigner ... to bathe
balcon, le ... balcony
balle, la ... ball
banane, la ... banana
banc, le ... bench
banlieue, la ... suburbs
banque, la ... bank
bas ... low
en bas ... below, downstairs
basé ... based
bateau, le ... boat
beau ... beautiful
beaucoup ... many, a lot
belle ... beautiful
beurre, le ... butter
bicyclette, la ... bicycle
bien ... well
pas bien ... not too well
bien sûr ... of course
bière, la ... beer
bijouterie, la ... jewelry
billet, le ... airplane/train ticket
billet de banque, le ... banknote
bistro, le ... restaurant
blanc, blanche ... white
blanchisserie, la ... laundry
bleu (e) ... blue
blouse, la ... blouse
boeuf, le ... beef
boire ... to drink
bois, les ... woods
boisson, la ... beverage
boîte aux lettres, la ... mailbox
bon/bonne ... good
bon appétit ... enjoy your meal
bonbon, le ... candy
bonjour ... good morning, good afternoon
bonne chance ... good luck
bonne nuit ... good night
bonsoir ... good evening
botte, la ... boot
boucherie, la ... butcher's shop
boulangerie, la ... bakery
bouteille, la ... bottle
boutique, la ... shop
brasserie, la ... beer-saloon, restaurant
bref ... brief, short
brosse à dents, la ... toothbrush
brouillard, le ... fog
bureau, le ... desk, office
bureau de change, le ... money-exchange counter

C

ça ... that, it
cabine téléphonique, la ... telephone booth
cabinets, les ... toilets
café, le ... cafe
café au lait ... coffee and steamed milk
caisse, la ... cashier, register
calendrier, le ... calender
canapé, le ... sofa
car ... for
car, le ... bus
carte, la ... map
carte postale, la ... postcard
cathédrale, la ... cathedral
catholique ... Catholic
ce, cette ... that, this
ceinture, la ... belt
cendrier, le ... ashtray
cent ... one hundred
centime, le ... centime
centre, le ... center
cerise, la ... cherry
ces ... these, those
c'est ... it is
chaise, la ... chair
chambre, la ... room
chambre à coucher, la ... bedroom
chandail, le ... sweater
changement, le ... change
changer (de train, d'autobus) ... to transfer, exchange (money)
chapeau, le ... hat
charcuterie, la ... delicatessen
chat, le ... cat
château, le ... castle
chaud (e) ... hot
chaussette, la ... sock
chaussure, la ... shoe
chef, le ... cook
chemise, la ... shirt
chemise de nuit, la ... nightshirt
chèque, le ... bank check
cher, chère ... expensive
cheveux, les ... hair
chien, le ... dog
cinquante ... fifty
clé, la ... key
coiffeur, le ... hairdresser
coin, le ... corner
colis, le ... package
combien ... how much
combinaison, la ... slip (undergarment)
commander ... to order
commencer ... to begin
comment ... how
commissariat de police, le ... police station
compagnie, la ... company
compartiment, le ... compartment
complet, le ... suit (clothes)
composer ... compose, dial (a telephone)
comprendre ... to understand
compris ... included
concierge, le/la ... doorkeeper
conducteur, le ... the driver
conduire ... to drive
confiserie, la ... confectionery
confiture, la ... jam
continuer ... to continue
contravention, la ... ticket
contrôleur, le ... ticket collector
corbeille à papier, la ... wastebasket
correspondences, les ... connections
côté, le ... side
à côté de ... beside, near, next to
couchette, la ... berth
couleur, la ... color
couloir, le ... hallway
couper ... to cut
courrier, le ... mail
court (e) ... short
cousin, le ... cousin (male)
cousine, la ... cousin (female)
coûte/coûter ... costs/to cost
couteau, le ... knife
coutume, la ... custom, habit
couverture, la ... blanket
cravate, la ... necktie
crayon, le ... pencil
crémerie, la ... dairy
cristal, le ... crystal
croissant, le ... crescent roll
cueillir ... to pick
cuiller, la ... spoon
cuisine, la ... kitchen
cuisinière, la ... stove
cuit (e) ... cooked
cuit au four ... baked

D

dame, la . . . . . . lady
dans . . . . . . in
danse, la . . . . . . dance
de . . . . . . of, from
de, de l', de la, des, du . . . . . . some
décembre, le . . . . . . December
déclaration, la . . . . . . declaration
défense d'entrer . . . . . . do not enter
degré, le . . . . . . degree
déjà . . . . . . already
  déjà vu . . . . . . already seen
délicieux, délicieuse . . . . . . delicious
demain . . . . . . tomorrow
  à demain . . . . . . till tomorrow
demander . . . . . . ask, ask for
demi (e) . . . . . . half
départ, le . . . . . . departure
derrière . . . . . . behind
désir, le . . . . . . desire
deux . . . . . . two
devant . . . . . . in front of
d'ici . . . . . . from here
dictionnaire, le . . . . . . dictionary
difficile . . . . . . difficult
dimanche, le . . . . . . Sunday
dire . . . . . . to say
dit/dire . . . . . . says/to say
dix . . . . . . ten
dix-huit . . . . . . eighteen
dix-neuf . . . . . . nineteen
dix-sept . . . . . . seventeen
docteur, le . . . . . . doctor
donc . . . . . . therefore, so
dormir . . . . . . to sleep
douce . . . . . . fresh (water), sweet, soft
doucement . . . . . . softly, gently
douche, la . . . . . . shower
douze . . . . . . twelve
drap de bain, le . . . . . . bath sheet

E

eau, la . . . . . . water
école, la . . . . . . school
écrire . . . . . . to write
église, la . . . . . . church
elle . . . . . . it, she
elles . . . . . . they
en . . . . . . in
encore . . . . . . again, still
enfants, les . . . . . . children
entre . . . . . . between
entrée, la . . . . . . entry
  entrée interdite . . . . . . do not enter
  entrée latérale . . . . . . side entry
  entrée principale . . . . . . main entry
entrées, les . . . . . . main dishes
entrer . . . . . . to go in, enter
envoyer . . . . . . to send
escalier, le . . . . . . stairs
escalier roulant, le . . . . . . escalator
Espagne, la . . . . . . Spain
essence, la . . . . . . gasoline
est, le . . . . . . east
est/être . . . . . . is/to be
est-ce . . . . . . is it
et . . . . . . and
étage, le . . . . . . floor, story
état, le . . . . . . state
  Etats-Unis d'Amérique, les . . . . . . USA
était . . . . . . was
été, le . . . . . . summer
êtes/être . . . . . . are/to be
étranger, étrangère . . . . . . foreign
Europe, la . . . . . . Europe
européen, européenne . . . . . . European
excusez-moi . . . . . . excuse me
exemple, le . . . . . . example
extrêmement . . . . . . extremely

F

F . . . . . . abbrev. for franc
facile . . . . . . easy
faim, la . . . . . . hunger
faire . . . . . . to do/make
faire un appel . . . . . . to telephone
famille, la . . . . . . family
farci (e) . . . . . . stuffed
femme, la . . . . . . woman
fenêtre, la . . . . . . window
fermé (e) . . . . . . closed
fête, la . . . . . . feast, festival
feuille, la . . . . . . sheet of paper
février, le . . . . . . February
fille, la . . . . . . girl, daughter
fils, le . . . . . . son
fin, la . . . . . . end
fleur, la . . . . . . flower
fleuriste, le . . . . . . florist
foi, la . . . . . . faith
football, le . . . . . . soccer
forêt, la . . . . . . forest
forme, la . . . . . . form, shape
formuler . . . . . . to formulate
fort (e) . . . . . . loudly
foyer, le . . . . . . hearth, lobby
frais . . . . . . fresh, cool
franc, le . . . . . . franc
français (e) . . . . . . French
Français, les . . . . . . the French people
France, la . . . . . . France
fréquence, la . . . . . . frequency
frère, le . . . . . . brother
frit (e) . . . . . . fried
froid (e) . . . . . . cold
fruit, le . . . . . . fruit
fumer . . . . . . to smoke

G

gant de toilette, le . . . . . . wash glove
garage, le . . . . . . garage
garçon, le . . . . . . boy, waiter
gare, la . . . . . . train station
gâteau, le . . . . . . cake
gauche . . . . . . left
  à gauche . . . . . . to the left
généralement . . . . . . generally
gibier, le . . . . . . wild game
glace, la . . . . . . mirror, ice, ice cream
gouvernement, le . . . . . . government
grand (e) . . . . . . large, tall
grand-mère, la . . . . . . grandmother
grand-père, le . . . . . . grandfather
grande serviette, la . . . . . . large towel
grands-parents, les . . . . . . grandparents
grillé (e) . . . . . . grilled
gris (e) . . . . . . gray
gros, grosse . . . . . . thick, big
guichet, le . . . . . . counter, window

H

habiter . . . . . . to live, reside
haut (e) . . . . . . high
  en haut . . . . . . above
heure, la . . . . . . hour
hier . . . . . . yesterday
hiver, le . . . . . . winter
homme, le . . . . . . man
horaire, le . . . . . . timetable
horloge, la . . . . . . large clock
horlogerie, la . . . . . . clock and watchmaker's shop
hors-d'oeuvre, le . . . . . . appetizer
hôtel, le . . . . . . hotel
hôtelier, le . . . . . . hotelkeeper
huit . . . . . . eight

I

ici . . . . . . here
idée, la . . . . . . idea
identique . . . . . . identical
il . . . . . . it, he
île, la . . . . . . island
il faut . . . . . . it is necessary
il n'y a pas de quoi . . . . . . you're welcome/it's nothing
ils . . . . . . they
image, la . . . . . . picture
imperméable, le . . . . . . raincoat
important (e) . . . . . . important
indicatif régional, le . . . . . . area code
industrie, la . . . . . . industry
ingénieur, le . . . . . . engineer
institut, le . . . . . . institute
interdit (e) . . . . . . prohibited
intéressant (e) . . . . . . interesting
intérêt, le . . . . . . interest
intérieur, le . . . . . . inside, interior
  à l'intérieur . . . . . . within
introduire . . . . . . introduce, insert
Irelande, la . . . . . . Ireland
Italie, la . . . . . . Italy
italien, italienne . . . . . . Italian

J

jambon, le . . . . . . ham
janvier, le . . . . . . January
Japon, le . . . . . . Japan
japonais (e) . . . . . . Japanese
jaquette, la . . . . . . woman's jacket
jardin, le . . . . . . garden
jaune . . . . . . yellow
je I
jeton, le . . . . . . token for telephone calls
jeudi, le . . . . . . Thursday
jeunesse, la . . . . . . young people, youth
jouet, le . . . . . . toy
jour, le . . . . . . day
journal, le . . . . . . newspaper
juif, juive . . . . . . Jewish
juillet, le . . . . . . July
juin, le . . . . . . June
jupe, la . . . . . . skirt
jus, le . . . . . . juice
  jus d'orange . . . . . . orange juice
juste . . . . . . just, fair, right

K

kilo, le . . . . . . kilo
kilomètre, le . . . . . . kilometer
kiosque, le . . . . . . newsstand

L

la, l', le, les . . . . . . the
lac, le . . . . . . lake
lait, le . . . . . . milk
laiterie, la . . . . . . dairy
lampe, la . . . . . . lamp
langage, le . . . . . . language
lavabo, le . . . . . . washbasin
laver . . . . . . to wash
leçon, la . . . . . . lesson
lecture, la . . . . . . reading
légume, le . . . . . . vegetable
lent (e) . . . . . . slow
lentement . . . . . . slowly
lettre, la . . . . . . letter
liberté, la . . . . . . liberty
librairie, la . . . . . . bookstore
libre . . . . . . free
lieu, le . . . . . . place
ligne, la . . . . . . line
limonade, la . . . . . . lemonade
linge, le . . . . . . linens
lingerie, la . . . . . . underclothing
lire . . . . . . to read

liste, la .... list
lit, le .... bed
wagon-lit, le .... sleeping car
litre, le .... liter
living-room, le .... living room
livre, le .... book
local (e) .... local
appel local, le .... local call
logement, le .... lodging
long, longue .... long
lorsque .... when
louer .... to rent
voiture à louer, la .... rental car
lumière, la .... light
lundi, le .... Monday
lunettes, les .... spectacles

M

Madame .... Mrs.
Mademoiselle .... Miss
magasin, le .... store
grand magasin, le .. department store
magazine, le .... magazine
magnifique .... magnificent
mai, le .... May
maillot de bain, le .... swimsuit
main, la .... hand
sac à main, le .... handbag
maintenant .... now
mais .... but
maison, la .... house
majorité, la .... majority
mal .... poorly, badly
pas mal .... not too bad
malade .... sick
manger .... to eat
manteau, le .... coat
marchand, le .... merchant
marché, le .... market
bon marché .... cheap, inexpensive
marché aux puces .... flea market
mardi, le .... Tuesday
marron .... brown
mars, le .... March
matin, le .... morning
mauvais (e) .... bad
menu, le .... menu
mer, la .... sea
Mer du nord, la .... The North Sea
merci .... thank you
mercredi, le .... Wednesday
mère, la .... mother
messieurs, les .... gentlemen
mètre, le .... meter
métro, métropolitan, le .... subway
meuble, le .... furniture
mieux .... better
mille .... one thousand
mince .... thin
minute, la .... minute
miroir, le .... mirror
mode, la .... fashion
à la mode .... fashionable
moins .... less
moins le quart .... a quarter to
mois, le .... the month
moment, le .... moment
monde, le .... world
tout le monde .... everyone
monnaie, la .... coins, money
montagne, la .... mountain
monter .... to board/climb
montre, la .... watch
montrer .... to show
mot, le .... word
mousse, la .... whipped cream, froth
moutarde, la .... mustard
mouton, le .... mutton
multicolore .... multi-colored
mur, le .... wall

musée, le .... museum
muselman (e) .... Moslem
musique, la .... music

N

nation, la .... nation
nature, la .... nature
ne. . . .pas, n'. . . .pas .... no, not
n'est-ce pas? .... isn't it?
nécessaire .... necessary
nécessité, la .... necessity
neige (il neige) .... it is snowing
neuf .... nine
neuf, neuve .... new
Noël .... Christmas
noir (e) .... black
nom, le .... name
nombre, le .... number
non .... no
nord, le .... north
normal (e) .... normal
Norvège, la .... Norway
note, la .... bill in hotel
nous .... we
nouveau, nouvelle .... new
novembre, le .... November
nuit, la .... night
numéro, le .... number

O

obligatoire .... compulsory
objet, le .... object
occupé (e) .... busy, occupied
odeur, la .... smell
oeuf, le .... egg
oeuf mollet .... soft-boiled egg
oeufs à la coque .... boiled eggs
oeufs brouillés .... scrambled eggs
on .... one, people, they, we
On fait ça .... one does that
On dit que .... they say that
oncle, le .... uncle
ont/avoir .... have/to have
onze .... eleven
optimiste .... optimistic
orange, la .... orange
orchestre, le .... orchestra
ordinaire .... ordinary
oreiller, le .... pillow
organisé (e) .... organized
Orient, le .... Orient
où .... where
ou .... or
oublier .... to forget
ouest, le .... west
oui .... yes
outil, le .... tool, implement
ouvert (e) .... open
ouvrez/ouvrir .... open/to open

P

page, la .... page
paiement, le .... payment
pain, le .... bread
paire, la .... pair
pamplemousse, la .... grapefruit
pantalon, le .... pair of trousers
pantoufle, la .... slipper
papeterie, la .... stationer's
papier, le .... paper
papier-monnaie, le .... bills
paquet, le .... package
par .... by, per
par avion .... airmail
paragraphe, le .... paragraph
parapluie, le .... umbrella
parc, le .... park
pardon .... excuse me

parent, le .... parent, relative
parfait (e) .... perfect
C'est parfait .... that's fine
parfumerie, la .... perfumery
parler .... to speak
partir .... to leave
pas bien .... not too well
pas mal .... not too bad
passe/passer .... happens/to happen
passeport, le .... passport
pâtisserie, la .... pastry, pastry shop
pauvre .... poor
payer .... to pay
P.C.V .... collect call
peigne, le .... comb
pellicule, la .... film
pelouse, la .... grass
pendule, la .... clock
perdre .... to lose
père, le .... father
personnes, les .... people
petit déjeuner, le .... breakfast
petit (e) .... small
peu .... little
peuple, le .... people
pharmacie, la .... pharmacy
photo, la .... photo, photograph
appareil photo, le .... camera
phrase, la .... sentence
pièce, la .... room, piece
pièce de monnaie, la .... coin
pied, le .... foot
pile, la .... battery
pilule, la .... pill
piscine, la .... pool
placard, le .... cupboard, closet
place, la .... seat, place
plafond, le .... ceiling
plage, la .... beach
plaisir, le .... pleasure
avec plaisir .... with pleasure
plan, le .... map
pleut (il pleut) .... it is raining
plus .... more
pointure, la ...... size (shoes and gloves)
poisson, le .... fish
poissonnerie, la .... fish market
poivre, le .... pepper
Pôle nord, le .... North Pole
Pôle sud, le .... South Pole
police, la .... police
politesse, la .... politeness
pomme, la .... apple
porc, le .... pork
porte, la .... door
portefeuille, le .... wallet
poste, la .... mail
bureau de poste, le .... post office
P et T .... post office
potage, le .... soup
pour .... for
pourboire, le .... tip
pourquoi .... why
pouvoir .... to be able to/can
pratique .... practical
premier, première .... first
préparer .... to prepare
préposition, la .... preposition
près d'ici .... near to here
printemps, le .... spring
prix, le .... price
problème, le .... problem
prochain (e) .... next
prolonger .... to lengthen
propre .... clean
protestant (e) .... Protestant
puis .... then
pull, le .... sweater
pyjama, le .... pajama

Q

quai, le .... platform
quand .... when
quarante .... forty
quart, le .... a quarter
  et quart .... a quarter past
  moins le quart .... a quarter to
quatorze .... fourteen
quatre .... four
quatre-vingt-dix .... ninety
quatre-vingts .... eighty
que, qu' .... what, that
qu'est-ce que c'est? .... what is it
quel, quelle .... what, which
Quelle heure est-il? ..... What time is it?
question, la .... question
qui .... who, what
quincaillerie, la .... hardware store
quinze .... fifteen

R

radio, la .... radio
rasoir, le .... razor
rapide .... fast
Rapide, le (RAP) .... train
rapidement .... quickly
rayon, le .... department
récepteur, le .... receiver
recette, la .... recipe, receipt
réciter .... to recite
reçu, le .... receipt
réfrigérateur, le .... refrigerator
religion, la .... religion
renseignements, les .... information
  bureau de renseignements, le .... information office
repas, le .... meal
répéter .... to repeat
répondre .... to reply, answer
réponse, la .... answer
rendez-vous, le .... appointment
réservation, la .... reservation
réserver .... to reserve/to book
restaurant, le .... restaurant
restaurant routier, le .... truck stop
reste, le .... rest, remaining
rester .... to remain, stay
retard, le .... delay
  en retard .... late
réveil, le .... alarm clock
revue, la .... magazine
rez-de-chaussée, le .... ground floor
riche .... rich
rideau, le .... curtain
rien (ne) .... nothing
robe, la .... dress
robe de chambre, la .... bathrobe
rose .... pink
rose, la .... rose
rôti (e) .... roasted
rouge .... red
route, la .... road
rue, la .... street
russe .... Russian

S

sac, le .... bag, sack
  sac à main, le .... handbag
saison, la .... season
salade, la .... salad
salle à manger, la .... dining room
salle d'attente, la .... waiting room
salle de bain, la .... bathroom
salut .... hi
salutations, les .... greetings
samedi, le .... Saturday
sandale, la .... sandal
sang, le .... blood
santé, la .... healthy
saucisse, la .... sausage
saucisson, le .... salami, sausage
savoir .... to know a fact
savon, le .... soap
second (e) .... second
seize .... sixteen
sel, le .... salt
semaine, la .... week
sept .... seven
septembre, le .... September
serveur, le .... waiter
serveuse, la .... waitress
service, le .... service
serviette, la .... napkin, towel
  grande serviette, la .... large towel
seulement .... only
signalisations, les .... signs
s'il vous plaît .... please
similarité, la .... similarity
simple .... simple, single, ordinary
six .... six
slip, le .... underpants
SNCF .... French national railroad
soeur, la .... sister
soir, le .... evening
soixante .... sixty
soixante-dix .... seventy
soleil, le .... sun
somme, la .... sum
sonnette, la .... doorbell
sont/être .... are/to be
sortie, la .... exit
  sortie de secours, la ... emergency exit
  sortie principale, la .... main exit
sortir .... to go out
soulier, le .... shoe
soupe, la .... soup
sous .... under
sous-sol, le .... basement
soutien-gorge, le .... brassiere
souvenir, le .... souvenir
souvent .... often
specialité de la maison, la .... specialty of the house
sport, le .... sport
standardiste, le .... the operator
station d'essence, la .... gas station
stopper .... to stop
stylo, le .... pen
sucre, le .... sugar
sud, le .... South
Suède, la .... Sweden
suis/être .... am/to be
Suisse, la .... Switzerland
suivant (e) .... following
supérieur (e) .... superior, upper
supermarché, le .... supermarket
sur .... on
sympathique .... likeable, nice
système, le .... system

T

tabac, le .... tobacco
table, la .... table
tableau, le .... picture
taille, la .... size (clothing)
tailleur, le .... tailor
tante, la .... aunt
tapis, le .... carpet
tapisserie, la .... tapestry, wallpaper
tarte, la .... pie
tarte aux pommes, la .... apple pie
taxe, la .... tax, charge
taxi, le .... taxi
télégramme, le .... telegram
téléphone, le .... telephone
téléphoner .... to telephone
téléphoniste, le .... operator
télévision, la .... television
température, la .... temperature
temps, le .... weather, time
terrasse, la .... terrace, sidewalk
tête, la .... head
thé, le .... tea
théâtre, le .... theater
thermomètre, le .... thermometer
ticket, le .... ticket
toilettes, les .... toilets
tour, la .... tower
tourner .... to turn
tout droit .... straight ahead
train, le .... train
transport, le .... transportation
treize .... thirteen
trente .... thirty
très .... very
trois .... three
troisième .... third
trouver .... to find
typique .... typical

U

un (e) .... a, one
unique .... sole, only, single

V

vacances, les .... vacation, holiday
vais/aller .... go/to go
vaisselle, la .... dishes
valise, la .... suitcase
vanille, la .... vanilla
variété, la .... variety
veau, le .... veal, calf
vendre .... to sell
venir .... to come
vent, le .... wind
vente, la .... sale
verbe, le .... verb
verre, le .... glass
vert (e) .... green
veston, le .... man's jacket
vêtement, le .... clothes
veuillez .... would you please
viande, la .... meat
vie, la .... life
vient/venir .... comes/to come
vierge, la .... virgin
vieux, vieille .... old
vigne, la .... grape vine
ville, la .... city
vin, le .... wine
vingt .... twenty
violet/violette .... violet
visite, la .... visit
vite .... fast
vocabulaire, le .... vocabulary
voie, la .... track
voilà .... there is/there are
voir .... to see
voiture, la .... car
  voiture à louer, la .... rental car
volaille, la .... poultry
votre .... your
voudrais .... would like
voudrions .... would like
vouloir .... to want
vous .... you
voyage, le .... trip, travel
  agence de voyage, la .... travel agency
  Bon voyage! .... have a good trip
voyageur, le .... traveler

W

wagon, le .... railroad car
wagon-lit, le .... sleeping car
wagon-restaurant, le .... dining car
W.C., le .... water closet, toilet

Y

y a-t-il .... are there/is there?

DRINKING GUIDE

This guide is intended to explain the sometimes overwhelming variety of beverages available to you while in France. It is by no means complete. Some of the experimenting has been left up to you, but this should get you started. The asterisks (*) indicate brand names.

BOISSONS CHAUDES (hot drinks)

café noir	coffee, black
café au lait	coffee with milk
café crème	coffee with cream
café express	expresso
café filtre	filtered coffee
thé	tea
au citron	with lemon
au lait	with milk
chocolat	hot chocolate

BOISSONS FROIDES (cold drinks)

lait froid	cold milk
lait aromatisé	flavored milk
eau minérale	mineral water
***Vittel**	
***Perrier**	
***Vichy**	
limonade	lemonade
jus de fruits	fruit juice
jus d'orange	orange juice
jus de pomme	apple juice
jus de tomate	tomato juice
orange pressé	squeezed orange juice
citron pressé	squeezed lemon juice
cidre	cider
thé glacé	iced tea
café glacé	iced coffee

APÉRITIFS (aperitifs)

These may be enjoyed straight or over ice.

porto	port
xérès	sherry
Pineau de Charente	grape juice and cognac
Kir	Crème de Cassis and white wine
***Pernod/Pastis/Ricard**	anise base
***Campari**	***Martini blanc**
***Cinzano**	***Martini rouge**
***Dubonnet**	***St. Raphaël**

COGNAC (cognac)

Cognac is a special type of brandy and is only produced in the region of Cognac.

***Rémy Martin**	***St. Rémy**
***Courvoisier**	***Martell**
***Hennessy**	***Hine**

CHAMPAGNE (champagne)

Champagne only comes from the region of Champagne.

***Dom Perignon** (the monk who invented champagne)
***Mumms**
***Piper-Heidsieck**
***Taitinger**
***Moët et Chandon**
***Bollinger**

LA GLACE .... ice

BIÈRES (beers)

There are a variety of brands including both **blonde** (light) and **brune** (dark). **La bière** is purchased in **bouteille** (bottle) or **à la pression** (draught).

PRESSION (draught)

***Kronenbourg Export**

le demi	small glass
le baron	medium glass
la chope	tankard

BOUTEILLE (bottle)

***Kanterbrau**
***Kronenbourg**
***Pelforth brune**
***Tuborg**
***Paulaner**

VINS (wines)

The wine production in France is closely controlled by the government, making it much easier to know what you are buying. You may drink wine by the **verre** (glass), the **carafe** (carafe) or the **bouteille** (bottle).

vin rouge	red wine
vin blanc	white wine
vin rosé	rosé wine
vin mousseux	sparkling wine
vin ordinaire	table wine
vin de table	table wine
vin de la maison	the "house" wine
vin du pays	local wine of the region

A.O.C. (Appelation d'origine contrôlée) superior wine
V.D.Q.S. (Vins délimités de qualité supérieure) choice wine
Premier cru/Grand cru good vintage wine

The major wine-producing areas **de la France** are

Bordeaux	**Bourgogne**
Loire	**Côtes du Rhône**
Alsace	**Champagne**

ALCOOL (spirits)

Cocktail drinking is not wide-spread in France. The following are available in large, international hotels and **"Bars américains."**

gin	gin
vodka	vodka
rhum	rum
whiskey	scotch
bourbon	bourbon
martini dry	American martini

DIGESTIFS (liqueurs, brandies)

eau de vie	grain natural spirits
fine à l'eau	brandy and soda
***Drambuie**	***Armagnac**
***Cointreau**	***Chartreuse**
***Grand Marnier**	***Bénédictine**

Salades (salads)

laitue	lettuce salad
laitue chicorée	chicory
escarole	coarse-leafed green lettuce
endive belge	Belgian endive
mâche	wild field lettuce
romaine	romaine
mélangée	mixed
mimosa	green salad with egg yolks
mixte	mixed
niçoise	string beans, potatoes, tuna
verte	tossed green
de pissenlits	dandelion greens
de saison	seasonal
de tomates	tomato
vinaigrette	in vinegar and oil

Légumes (vegetables)

haricots verts	green string beans
haricots flageolets	small, pale green beans
petits pois	peas
lentilles	lentils
asperges	asparagus
carottes	carrots
épinards	spinach
poireaux	leeks
tomates	tomatoes
champignons	cultivated mushrooms
chanterelles	wild mushrooms
morilles	morel, wild mushrooms
chou	cabbage
chou-fleur	cauliflower
choux de Bruxelles	brussels sprouts
betteraves	beets
maïs	corn
concombres	cucumbers
navets	turnips
oignons	onions
radis	radishes
ail	garlic
artichauts	artichoke
aubergines	eggplant
courgettes	zucchini squash
macédoine des légumes	diced, cooked vegetables

FOLD HERE

Pommes de terre (potatoes)

croquettes	mashed, dipped and fried
gratin dauphinois	scalloped
frites	French fried
à l'anglaise	peeled and boiled
nature	plain boiled
maître d'hôtel	boiled and sautéed
purée	mashed
vapeur	steamed

Fruit (fruit)

pomme	apple
poire	pear
abricot	apricot
pêche	peach
banane	banana
orange	orange
mandarine	mandarin orange
cerise	cherry
prune	plum
pruneau	prune
melon	melon
pamplemousse	grapefruit
pastèque	watermelon
raisin	grape
raisin sec	raisin
grenade	pomegranate
ananas	pineapple
citron	lemon
compote de fruits	stewed fruits

Baies (berries)

fraise	strawberry
framboise	raspberry
mûre	blackberry
groseille à maquereau	gooseberry
groseille (rouge, blanche)	red or white currant
cassis	black currant
myrtille	bilberry
airelle	blueberry

Bon appétit!

FOLD HERE

La Carte

Préparation (preparation)

cuit	cooked
cru	raw
rôti	roasted
frit	fried
cuit au four	baked
grillé	grilled
farci/fourré	stuffed or filled
bouilli	boiled
fumé	smoked
mariné	marinated
braisé	braised
en croûte	cooked in crust
en cocotte	cooked in earthenware
au gratin	sprinkled with cheese
au lard	cooked in salt pork
au jus	cooked in its own juice
bleu	extremely rare
saignant	rare
à point	medium rare
bien cuit	well done

Autres (others)

confiture	jam
miel	honey
sel	salt
poivre	pepper
huile	oil
vinaigre	vinegar
moutarde	mustard
riz	rice
pain	bread
baguette	long loaf of bread
nouilles	noodles
pâtes	pasta
fromage	cheese
dessert	dessert
gâteau	cake
pâtisserie	pastry
glace	ice cream
chantilly	whipped cream
yaourt	yoghurt

Hors-d'oeuvres (hors d'oeuvres)

huîtres	oysters
assiette de charcuterie	assorted sausages, salamis
céleri-rave rémoulade	celery root in sauce
coeur de palmier	hearts of palm
crudités	raw vegetables
escargots	snails
foie gras truffé	goose liver with truffles
jambon cru	raw-cured ham
langue de boeuf gelée	beef tongue with aspic
pâté de campagne	country style, coarse paté
salade panachée	mixed vegetable salad
saucisson	sausage/salami
terrine maison	house paté in terrine
croque monsieur	grilled ham and cheese sandwich
croque madame	grilled chicken and cheese sandwich

Potages, soupes (soups)

bisque	cream soup with seafood
bouillabaisse	rich fish soup
crème de tomates	cream of tomato
petite marmite	soup-stew
pistou	vegetable soup
soupe du jour	soup of the day
soupe à l'oignon	onion soup
consommé	clarified stock
soupe à la reine	chicken soup with rice
velouté de légumes	thick vegetable soup
vichyssoise	potato and leek soup

Oeufs (eggs)

à la coque	soft-boiled
mollet	medium boiled
brouillés	scrambled
dur	hard-boiled
poché	poached
omelette nature	plain omelette
omelette au fromage	cheese omelette
quiche	cheese and egg pie
. . .à cheval	. . .topped with a fried egg
au plat	fried (sometimes baked)

Viande (meat)

Veau (veal)

blanquette de veau	veal stew with gravy
côte de veau	veal chop
côtelette de veau	veal chop
foie de veau	calf's liver

FOLD HERE

Viande (meat) continued

fricassée de veau	veal stew
jarret de veau	veal shank
médaillons de veau	discs of pan-fried veal
noisette de veau	tenderloin morsels of veal
poitrine de veau farcie	stuffed breast of veal
ris de veau	veal sweetbreads
rognons de veau	veal kidneys
rôti de veau	roast veal
tendron de veau	braised breast of veal
tête de veau	head of veal
escalope de veau	veal cutlet

Boeuf (beef)

boeuf bourguignon	red wine stew
carbonades de boeuf	sautéed and braised slices
côte de boeuf	beef rib steaks
daube de boeuf	marinated pot-roast
entrecôte de boeuf	boneless beef rib steak
estouffade de boeuf	braised beef in wine stew
filet de boeuf	tenderloin of beef
langue de boeuf	beef tongue
médaillon de boeuf	thick discs of tenderloin
queue de boeuf	oxtail
braisé de boeuf	beef stew in wine
tournedos	beef tenderloin
terrine de boeuf	casserole stew
tripes	stomach lining
moelle	beef bone marrow

Porc (pork)

côte/côtelette de porc	pork chop
carré de porc provençal	rib loin roast with spices
cuissot de porc	fresh ham roast
jarret de porc	pork shank
noisette de porc	small tenderloin discs
pied de porc	pig's foot
rognons de porc	pork kidneys
rôti de porc	pork roast
tête de porc roulée	rolled pig's head
cochon au lait	suckling pig (roasted)

Agneau (lamb)

carré d'agneau	lamb rib roast
côte/côtelette d'agneau	lamb chop
épaule d'agneau	lamb shoulder
gigot d'agneau	leg of lamb
cervelle d'agneau	lamb's brains

FOLD HERE

Volaille (poultry)

poulet	chicken
coq au vin	chicken in wine sauce
canard	duck
caneton	duckling
chapon	capon
caille	quail
oie	goose
faisan	pheasant
pigeon	pigeon
dinde	turkey

Gibier (wild game)

gigue de chevreuil	roast leg of venison
bécasse	woodcock
escalope de sanglier	cutlets of wild boar
cuissot de marcassin	roast leg of wild pig
râble de lapin	saddle of rabbit
lapin sauté chasseur	rabbit sautéed in wine

Poissons et fruits de mer (fish and seafood)

anchois	anchovies
anguille	eel
cabillaud	codfish
calamar	squid
carpe	carp
colin	hake
coquillages	shellfish
coquilles Saint-Jacques	scallops
crabe	crab
crevettes	shrimps
écrevisses	fresh-water crayfish
flétan	halibut
grenouille	frog
hareng	herring
homard	true lobster, with claws
langouste	spiny lobster, no claws
langoustine	shellfish
morue	dried codfish
moules	mussels
oursins	sea urchins
perche	perch
poulpe	small octopus
quenelles	cylindrical fish dumpling
rouget de roche	Mediterranean red mullet
saumon	salmon
sole	sole
truite	trout
thon	tuna

(vuh-neer) **venir**	*(saw-puh-lay)* **s'appeler**
(ah-lay) **aller**	*(ah-shuh-tay)* **acheter**
(ah-vwahr) **avoir**	*(par-lay)* **parler**
(ah-prah$^{(n)}$-druh) **apprendre**	*(ah-bee-tay)* **habiter**
(zhuh) (voo-dray) **je voudrais**	*(ko-mah$^{(n)}$-day)* **commander**
(ah-vwahr) (buh-zwa$^{(n)}$) (duh) **avoir besoin de**	*(reh-stay)* **rester**

to be called	to come
to buy	to go
to speak	to have
to live/reside	to learn
to order	I would like
to stay/remain	to need

(deer) **dire**	*(vah$^{(n)}$-druh)* **vendre**
(mah$^{(n)}$-zhay) **manger**	*(vwahr)* **voir**
(bwahr) **boire**	*(ah$^{(n)}$-vwhy-ay)* **envoyer**
(ah-tah$^{(n)}$-druh) **attendre**	*(door-meer)* **dormir**
(koh$^{(n)}$-prah$^{(n)}$-druh) **comprendre**	*(troo-vay)* **trouver**
(ray-pay-tay) **répéter**	*(fare)* **faire**

to sell	to say
to see	to eat
to send	to drink
to sleep	to wait
to find	to understand
to do/make	to repeat

(ay-kreer) **écrire**	*(leer)* **lire**
(moh(n)-tray) **montrer**	*(vwhy-ah-zhay)* **voyager**
(pay-yay) **payer**	*(trah-vhy-ay)* **travailler**
(poo-vwahr) **pouvoir**	*(prah(n)-druh lah-vee-oh(n))* **prendre l'avion**
(duh-vwahr) **devoir**	*(eel) (foh)* **il faut**
(sah-vwahr) **savoir**	*(fare) (vah-leez)* **faire la valise**

to read	to write
to travel	to show
to work	to pay
to fly	to be able to/can
it is necessary	to have to/must/owe
to pack	to know

(koh-mah(n)-say) **commencer**	*(prah(n)-druh)* **prendre**
(oov-rear) **ouvrir**	*(moh(n)-tay)* **monter**
(fare) *(kwee-zeen)* **faire la cuisine**	*(day-sah(n)-druh)* **descendre**
(ah-tair-ear) **atterrir**	*(day-bar-kay)* **débarquer**
(ray-zair-vay) **réserver**	*(shah(n)-zhay)* *(duh)* **changer de. . .**
(koo-tay) **coûter**	*(ah-ree-vay)* **arriver**

to take	to begin
to climb/board	to open
to go down/get out	to cook
to disembark	to land
to transfer	to book/reserve
to arrive	to cost

(par-teer) **partir**	*(fair-may)* **fermer**
(koh(n)-dweer) **conduire**	*(lah-vay)* **laver**
(few-may) **fumer**	*(shah(n)-zhay)* **changer**
(duh-mah(n)-day) **demander**	*(pair-druh)* **perdre**
(eel) (nehzh) **il neige**	*(zhuh) (swee)* **je suis**
(eel) (pluh) **il pleut**	*(new) (sohm)* **nous sommes**

to close	to depart/leave
to wash	to drive
to exchange	to smoke
to lose	to ask
I am	it is snowing
we are	it is raining

(eel) il / (ell) elle } (ay) est	(oh) (bah) **haut - bas**
(voo-zet) **vous êtes**	(poh-vruh) (reesh) **pauvre - riche**
(eel) ils / (ell) elles } (soh(n)) sont	(koor) (loh(n)) **court - long**
(oh) (ruh-vwahr) **au revoir**	(mah-lahd) **malade -** (ah(n)) (bun) (form) **en bonne forme**
(eel-ee-ah) **il y a**	(boh(n)) (mar-shay) (share) **bon marché - cher**
(ko-mah(n)) (tah-lay-voo) **Comment allez-vous?**	(vee-yuh) (zhun) **vieux - jeune**

high - low	he she is
poor - rich	you are
short - long	they are
sick - healthy	good-bye
cheap - expensive	there is/there are
old - young	How are you?

(boh$^{(n)}$) (mow-vay) **bon - mauvais**	(veet) (rah-peed) (lah$^{(n)}$) **vite/rapide - lent**
(deuce-mah$^{(n)}$) (for) **doucement - fort**	(grow) (ma$^{(n)}$s) **gros - mince**
(grah$^{(n)}$) (puh-tee) **grand - petit**	(boh-koo) (duh) (puh) (duh) **beaucoup de - peu de**
(show) (fwah) **chaud - froid**	(oo-vair) (fair-may) **ouvert - fermé**
(gohsh) (dwah) **gauche - droit**	(doo) (ay-gruh) **doux - aigre**
(ah$^{(n)}$) (oh) (ah$^{(n)}$) (bah) **en haut - en bas**	(ek-skew-zay-mwah) (par-doh$^{(n)}$) **excusez-moi/pardon**

fast - slow	good - bad
thick - thin	soft - loud
much - little	large - small
open - closed	warm - cold
sweet - sour	left - right
excuse me	above - below

FRENCH

in 10 minutes a day®

by **Kristine Kershul**, M.A., University of California, Santa Barbara

adapted by Jan Fisher Brousseau

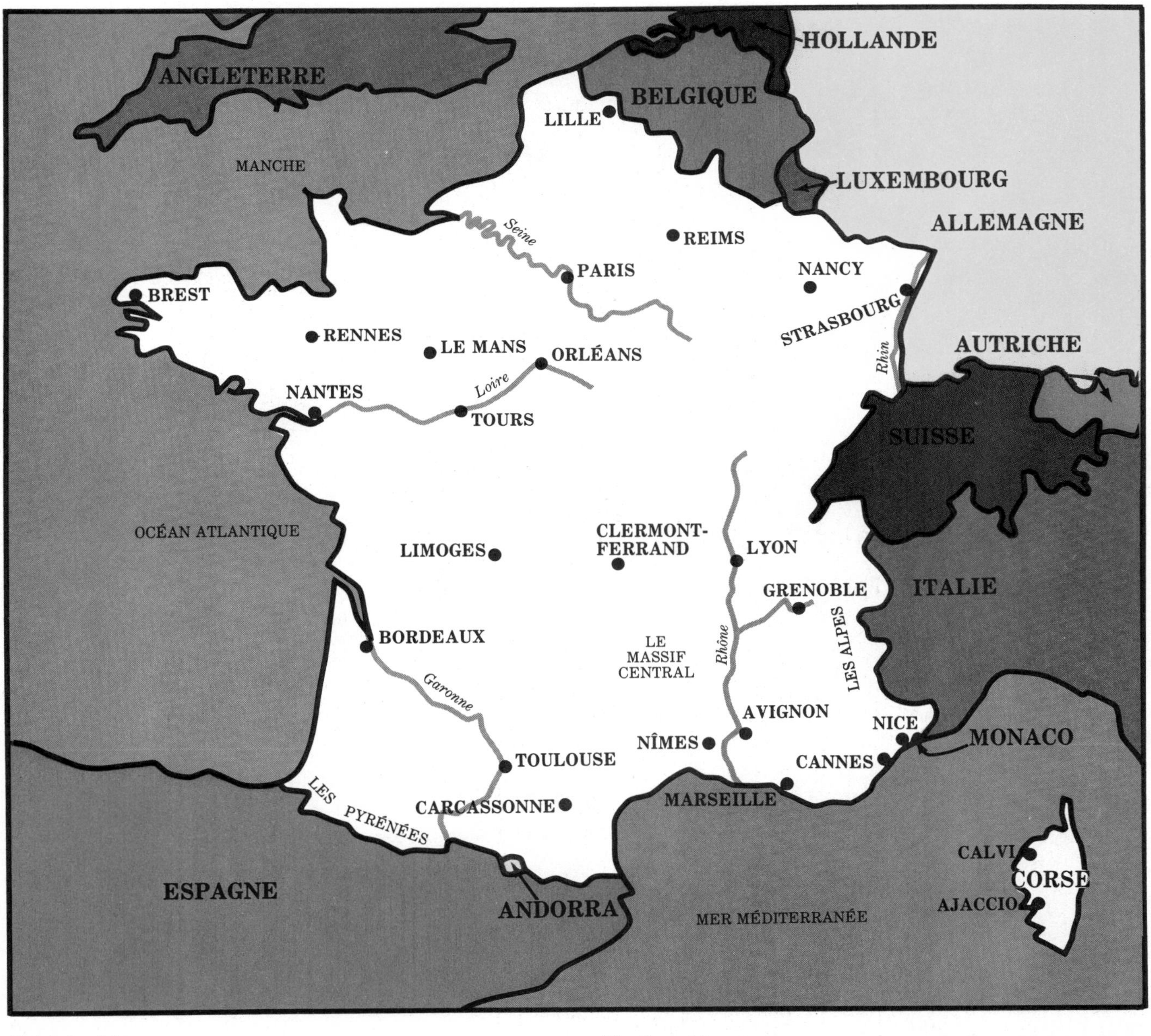

Published by
Bilingual Books, Inc.
6018 Seaview Avenue N.W.
Seattle, Washington 98107, U.S.A.
Telephone: (206) 789-7544
Telex: 499 6629 BBKS UI

Distributed by
USA: Cliffs Notes, Inc., Box 80728, Lincoln, Nebraska 68501
UK: Ruskin Book Services, 15 Comberton Hill, Kidderminster, Worcestershire DY10 1QG

 Sixth edition: printed 1987
(ISBN 0-916682-96-X)

L'alphabet
(ahl-fah-bay)

Many French letters sound the same as in English, but some French letters are pronounced or written differently. To learn the French sounds of these letters, write each example in the space provided in addition to saying the word many times. After you practice the word see if you can locate it on the map.

French letter	English sound	Example	*(Write it here)*
a	ah	**Paris** *(pah-ree)*	
au/eau	oh/oe	**Bordeaux** *(bore-doe)*	
c *(before, a,o,u)*	k	**Carcassonne** *(kar-kah-sohn)*	
c *(before e,i,y)*	s	**Nice** *(nees)*	
ç	s	**Alençon** *(ah-lah$^{(n)}$-soh$^{(n)}$)*	
ch	sh	**Champagne** *(shah$^{(n)}$-pahn-yuh)*	
e	uh	**Le Mans** *(luh mah$^{(n)}$)*	
é	ay	**Orléans** *(or-lay-ah$^{(n)}$)*	
ei	eh	**Seine** *(sehn)*	
è/ê	e *(as in let)*	**Norvège** *(nor-vezh)*	
g *(before a,o,u)*	g	**Garonne** *(gar-own)*	
g *(before e,i,y)*	zh *(as in leisure)*	**Gironde** *(zhee-rohnd)*	
gn	ny *(as in onion)*	**Avignon** *(ah-veen-yoh$^{(n)}$)*	
i	ee	**Lille** *(leel)*	
j	zh	**Le Jura** *(luh zhew-rah)*	
o	oh	**Limoges** *(lee-mohzh)*	
qu	k	**Québec** *(kay-bek)*	
r	*(slightly rolled)*	**Rennes** *(ren)*	
s *(between vowels)*	z	**Toulouse** *(too-looz)*	
u	ew/ue	**Tunisie** *(tew-nee-zee)*	
x *(varies)*	gz	**Exeter** *(eg-zuh-tare)*	
	ks	**Luxembourg** *(lewk-sum-boor)*	
	s	**Auxerre** *(oh-sair)*	
y	ee	**Nancy** *(nah$^{(n)}$-see)*	

NASAL VOWEL SOUNDS

am, an, em, en	ah$^{(n)}$ *(taunt nasalized)*	**Angleterre** *(ah$^{(n)}$-gluh-tare)*	
im, in, aim, ain, ein, eim	a$^{(n)}$ *(than nasalized)*	**Reims** *(ra$^{(n)}$s)*	
om, on	oh$^{(n)}$ *(don't nasalized)*	**Toulon** *(too-loh$^{(n)}$)*	
um, un	uh$^{(n)}$ *(fun nasalized)*	**Melun** *(mel-uh$^{(n)}$)*	